your special wedding vows

sharon naylor

SOURCEBOOKS CASABLANCA™
AN IMPRINT OF SOURCEBOOKS, INC.®
NAPERVILLE, ILLINOIS

Published by Sourcebooks, Inc.
P.O. Box 4410, Naperville, Illinois 60567-4410
(630) 961-3900
FAX: (630) 961-2168
www.sourcebooks.com

Naylor, Sharon.
Your special wedding vows / by Sharon Naylor
    p. cm.
ISBN 1-4022-0267-9 (alk. paper)
1. Marriage service. I. Title.
BL619.M37N39 2004
392.5—dc22

                    2004000594

Printed and bound in the United States of America
QW 10 9 8 7 6 5 4 3 2 1

For Aunt Millie and Uncle Bill,
Who lived their wedding vows each day,
Who exemplified love, respect, and best friendship;
For blending together of all that they were,
And inspiring us all never to settle for less
Than True and Lasting Love.

ACKNOWLEDGMENTS

Words can barely express my gratitude to my editors at Sourcebooks, Hillel Black and Deb Werksman, who welcomed me into their home and gave me the opportunity to share these sentiments with you all. And a clink of champagne glasses to my steadfast and spectacular agent Meredith Bernstein.

With special thanks to my friends and family, my colleagues in the wedding industry, Deborah Roth, Reverend Frank Jude Boccio, Sarah Stitham, and the thousands of brides and grooms who have shared their Big Day stories with me over the years. It's a pleasure to be a part of the wedding world every day, and I thank you all for joining me in it.

CONTENTS

Introduction

While the big excitement of planning a wedding usually revolves around the gown, the cake, the flowers, the band, the crystal chandeliers, and the horse-drawn carriage ride to the church, the most important part of any wedding—the centerpiece of it all—is the wedding vows. After all, without the declaration of your love and commitment to one another, there wouldn't be anything to celebrate with all that cake and champagne!

Your wedding vows are the focus of the entire day. They're the most important words you'll speak or hear for perhaps the rest of your lives.

No wonder writing the vows completely freaks out many engaged couples. When they think about the *significance* of those words—how they're a binding commitment, the biggest promises of their lives—many couples just freeze.

* How do I find the right words to express what I'm feeling?
* What's the right thing to say?
* How do I keep from sounding like an idiot?
* How do I keep from passing out at the altar?
* Do I really want to promise to *obey* him?

You can work yourself into quite a frenzy when you're standing on the edge of this task and looking at it from all kinds of anxious angles. Yes, this *is* a monumental moment you're talking about, and the words you say will live on in immortality once they're captured on your wedding video and in everyone's memories of the day, including your own. You'll be speaking from the heart in front of perhaps hundreds of your friends and family...who wouldn't freak out about that?

Just relax. Right now, the concept of your vows might be a bit overwhelming, but once you dive in and get into it, I promise you'll find that the words will just start flowing, and you'll probably even have a hard time narrowing them down.

ARE YOU TRADITIONAL OR ARE YOU MODERN?

As you start thinking about your wedding vows, you're going to discover that you're standing right in the middle of two worlds. On one side, you have the world of the traditional, religious, handed-down-through-generations vows, perhaps the same ones your parents took at their weddings...and on the other side, you have a world of complete wedding vow freedom where you can quote Dr. Maya Angelou—or Dr. Seuss if you'd like—as you completely personalize your vows with your own values and words. Where you fit in between those two worlds depends solely on what *you* want your wedding vows to be.

Some couples love holding with tradition and speaking the words the church gives them. And some couples run far from the prescribed script. Others borrow a little from one religious script, add in a bit of poetry or a personal anecdote, and cap it off with a line from their favorite song. Since you picked up this book, I'm betting that you have at least *some* of the latter in your vows situation. You want to create what you'll say on your Big Day.

So, that said, read on to explore just some of the options out there in traditional religious vows, poetry, multicultural and interfaith wording, humor, and family-oriented phrases for blending families or honoring your relatives. Create a tapestry of sentiments and pledges that work for *you*, as the wedding vows you'll hold true to forever.

The Top 15 Rules of Smart Vow Creation

Let's get you started off on the right foot. Before you lock yourself away for a weekend and scratch out your first draft, keep the following smart rules in mind to save you time, make the job a bit easier, and keep you from doing too much unnecessarily:

1. Do your research. Read up on the scripts of your chosen religion's vows, those written by your friends or colleagues, poetry you'll find in anthologies and on the Internet. Collect samples so that you're familiar with the many different flavors and styles of today's vows. Even your

wedding coordinator can hand you samples of her previous clients' words.

2. Start early. This task is not to be left until the night before the wedding, since you'll be tired and stressed from all the wedding day countdown activities and hassles. Write them now while you're still blushing from your engagement and steeped in love and romance. Or, at the very least, get them done a few weeks before the wedding and leave yourself some time for last-second tweaking.

3. Decide as a couple whether you'll write your vows together or individually. Some couples choose to write one set of vows and each repeat them during the ceremony, while others like to surprise one another on the wedding day with the gift of the promises and pledges they've written.

4. Before you set off to write, whether together or apart, plan a quiet night in which you'll discuss what you're feeling and what you wish to promise to one another.

5. Be yourself. Don't try to fit some image of what you think you should sound like. If you're not one for the ultra-romantic flowery talk, don't rope yourself in (or get roped in) to talking like a lovesick Medieval knight or Gwyneth Paltrow in a Jane Austen adaptation movie. Stay true to your own style and tone, and make your words fit who you are.

6. Make room for a bit of humor and lightheartedness in your speech, as befitting your personality, but remember that this *is* a serious, sentimental

moment. So be serious where you have to be in honor of the solemnity of your ceremony rites.

7. Keep it short and sweet. Don't ramble on too long, but rather be concise and complete in what you say. There will be time later to express all you're feeling to one another.

8. Don't worry about going long with your first draft. The more the better in your first stages, so that you have plenty of material from which to find the true gems. Save your earlier drafts as a keepsake journal-type recording, or as a love letter to your intended.

9. Practice, practice, practice. Be sure to read your vow drafts out loud, since some phrases might come out more awkwardly in speech than in print. Once you hear yourself, you'll know better if it *feels* right.

10. Decide if you wish to memorize your vows, or print them out on cards for the officiant to read aloud and have you repeat. Some couples don't want to burden themselves with memorizing when they're sure they'll be nervous, so choose which form you prefer.

11. Choose key words carefully. Does "obey" make your hair stand on end? Have you ever said the word "cherish" before? Make sure the words you're using really nail your intentions. Use your computer's thesaurus for additional suggestions.

12. Make it your own. Use personal anecdotes (but not *too* personal) to make your vows your own.

13. Submit your vows to your officiant for his or her okay. Many houses of worship do retain strict rules about the wording of wedding ceremonies, and some officiants are going to be tougher than others about giving you complete creative control over your own promises. You might have to negotiate with an officiant, so start this process early on.

14. Give yourself permission to get emotional. For many couples, getting teary-eyed is a sign that they've gotten right to the heart of their sentiments.

15. Look your partner in the eye while you're reading your vows. This is an unforgettable moment, and these words are just for the two of you. They're your first and greatest gifts to each other as husband and wife, so deliver them well.

Getting Started: Your Wedding Vow Questionnaire

Grab your partner again for a glass of wine or two, maybe some great dessert, and spend some heart-to-heart time discussing the following questions in an effort to develop your thoughts for the vows *and* initiate the kind of soul-searching conversation that should start off every strong marriage. You'll find yourselves discussing some deep topics and divulging some strong feelings to one another, which is the best and wisest way to begin this task and your partnership. So set a time when you're both in the mood to talk so deeply, since it's important that you're both willing to give 100 percent to this discussion.

Ready? Here are your questions:

What did you think about each other when you first met?

When did you first know you were in love? Was there a specific moment, like when you saw him playing with his niece and nephew, or did it gradually evolve over time?

When did you first know you'd marry this person?

When and where did you first say "I Love You"?

Did others know you were in love before you both realized it or expressed it?

What do you love and admire most about the other person? (A top 10 list is fine here.)

What has your partner brought to your life that you didn't have before?

What characteristics and qualities do you think you developed as a result of being together?

What challenges did the two of you overcome during your time together that led you to this point in your relationship?

What does his/her family mean to you?

Are there any special moments that you shared with his/her family that stand out, that perhaps showed you more of your partner's depth and qualities?

What lessons about love and commitment have you learned from one another? From each other's families?

Who serves as your relationship role model, that couple with the deep love you wish to emulate? What is it about their relationship that you admire?

How do you see yourselves working through the challenges that lie ahead on the path of your life together?

What are five ways you'd describe your partner to your very best friend?

What do you promise to bring to your future children someday?

What are the five key ingredients to a successful marriage?

What are your goals, visions, and wishes for your future life together?

By now, you probably have a pretty clear idea of what's going to make it into your wedding vows, and you have plenty of time to refine them. So continue on through the collections in this book, and work through the creation of your own wedding vows, the very heart of your wedding day and your entire future together.

Part One:

The Traditional

Traditional Religious and Civil Ceremony Vow Scripts

You might find as you work with your chosen wedding officiant that the house of worship where you will marry has set guidelines for the vows you'll speak to one another. Some are more flexible than others in allowing you to play with and adapt the traditional, set-in-stone wording, so work with your officiant to blend just the right amount of modern touch and personalization into these time-honored scripts of religious vows. Some couples wish only to remove the *Thee's* and *Thou's*, while others embrace the custom of Old World wording and make no changes at all.

This is what makes choosing the right officiant *so* important. This expert of faith can guide you through the selection and personalization process, suggest readings and modifications that suit your own beliefs, and answer any and all of your questions.

As you read on through these collected religious vow scripts, please know that these are just a few of the many, many individual religious scripts out there. You'll perhaps see variations in the script your officiant hands you, and you might dig up additional variations in your additional research. Over time, individual lines have adapted to some degree, but most hold true to their roots.

I hope you won't limit yourself to just the wording of your own born or adopted faith. Read through the scripts of other religions' traditional vows, and you might discover a beautiful phrase or sentiment that you'd like to incorporate into your own vows. You might, for instance, borrow a poetic line from the Cherokee vows here, and add them to your Lutheran script alterations. The freedom to create meaningful vows with a faith-based angle is yours.

An Exploration of Your Faith

Wedding coordinator Sarah Stitham of www.charmedplaces.com has this to say about the writing of religious vows: "Often, when couples face the task of writing their vows and they are *not* very religious in nature, they start thinking more about their faith. If they're not connected to their church or their religion, they might ask a lot of questions of their officiant, do more research on their own, and in turn become newly interested in and more connected to the faith of their upbringing *or* the faith of their partner. So this task of writing religious vows can inspire a new connection to faith."

BAPTIST

Will you, ____, have ____ to be your wife? Will you love her, comfort and keep her, and forsaking all others remain true to her as long as you both shall live?

Groom answers, "I _____ take thee _____ to be my wife, and before God and these witnesses I promise to be a true and faithful husband."

The bride then repeats her version of these vows.

CATHOLIC

I, _____, take you, _____, for my lawful wife/husband, to have and to hold, from this day forward, for better, for worse, for richer, for poorer, in sickness and health, until death do us part.

CIVIL CEREMONY

Civil ceremony vows are among the most changeable. With no firm rules imposed by a house of worship, couples being married by a civil officiant such as a judge, mayor, or justice of the peace are free to create their own personally-worded vows. These civil officiants *will*, however, come prepared with a variation on the following standard civil vows.

I, _____, take you, _____, to be my husband/wife, to have and to hold from this day forward, in true partnership and bonded by love. I pledge you my loyalty, my heart, and my support forever and ever.

EASTERN ORTHODOX

As mentioned earlier, some Orthodox wedding ceremonies require that the bride and groom do *not* speak their vows aloud, but rather enact wedding rituals while the vows are read by the officiant. One such ritual might be the exchanging of rings three times to symbolize the Holy Trinity, and another is the ceremonial crowning during which crowns are placed on the couple's heads. When the priest removes the crowns and says the blessing, "Be Thou magnified, O Bridegroom," the vows are now sealed.

EPISCOPALIAN

In the name of God, I, _____, take you, _____ to be my husband/wife, to have and to hold from this day forward, for better, for worse, for richer, for poorer, in sickness and in health, to love and to cherish, until we are parted by death. This is my solemn vow.

JEWISH

As they exchange rings, the bride and groom say in Hebrew:

Behold, thou are consecrated unto me with this ring according to the Law of Moses and of Israel.

CONSERVATIVE JEWISH VOWS

Following the *Rabbinical Assembly Manual*, the following vows are most often read:

Rabbi (addressing the groom): Do you _____, take _____ to be your lawful wedded wife to love, to honor, and to cherish?

The groom answers with, "I do."

Rabbi (addressing the bride): Do you, _____, take _____ to be your lawful wedded husband to love, to honor, and to cherish?

The bride answers with, "I do."

Rabbi, to the groom: Do you, _____, put this ring upon the finger of your bride and say to her, "Be thou consecrated to me, as my wife, by this ring, according to the Law of Moses and of Israel?"

In a single ring ceremony, the Rabbi asks the bride to repeat: May this ring I receive from thee be a token of my having become thy wife according to the Law of Moses and of Israel.

If the couple is exchanging tokens in a double ring ceremony, the bride says, "This ring is a symbol that thou art my husband in accordance with the Law of Moses and Israel."

REFORMED JEWISH VOW ADDITIONS:
From that point, the Rabbi might add:

O God, supremely blessed, supreme in might and glory, guide and bless this groom and bride. Standing here in the presence of God, the Guardian of the home, ready to enter into the bond of wedlock, answer in the fear of God, and in the hearing of those assembled:

Do you, _____, of your own free will and consent take _____ to be your wife/husband and do you promise to love, honor, and cherish her/him throughout life?

Bride and groom answer, "I do."

LUTHERAN (1ST VERSION, SIMPLIFIED)

There are many types of Lutheran churches in the United States, some more formal than others. Here is an example of one of the phrasings traditionally used for vows.

I, ____, take you, ____, to be my husband/wife from this day forward, to join with you and share all that is to come, and I promise to be faithful to you until death parts us.

LUTHERAN (2ND VERSION)

I, ____, take you, ____, to be my husband/wife, and these things I promise you:

I will be faithful to you and honest with you;

I will respect, trust, help, and care for you;

I will share my life with you;

I will forgive you as we have been forgiven;

And I will try with you better to understand ourselves, the world, and God;

Through the best and the worst of what is to come as long as we live.

METHODIST (1ST VERSION)

In the name of God, I, ____, take you, ____, to be my husband/wife, to have and to hold from this day forward, for better, for worse, for richer, for poorer, in sickness and in health, to love and to cherish, until we are parted by death. This is my solemn vow.

MUSLIM

Some Muslim wedding ceremonies do *not* require the bride and groom to repeat their vows aloud, but rather they simply answer in the affirmative while the vows and prayers are read to them by their officiant. If they will speak their vows aloud, they might read as follows:

The bride says: I, _____, offer you myself in marriage in accordance with the instructions of the Holy Quar'an and the Holy Prophet, peace and blessings be upon Him. I pledge, in honesty and with sincerity, to be for you an obedient and faithful wife.

The groom says: I pledge, in honesty and sincerity, to be for you a faithful and helpful husband.

NATIVE AMERICAN (APACHE)

Native American sentiments are among the most popular growing trends in vow-creation. Read on to see the beauty of these readings and see if they capture your imagination as well.

Now you will feel no rain, for each of you will be shelter for the other. Now you will feel no cold, for each of you will be warmth to the other. Now there will be no loneliness, for each of you will be companion to the other. Now you are two persons, but there is only one life before you. May beauty surround you both in the journey ahead and through all the years. May happiness be your companion and your days together be good and long upon the earth.

Treat yourselves and each other with respect, and remind yourselves often of what brought you together. Give the highest priority to the tenderness, gentleness, and kindness that your connection deserves. When frustration, difficulties, and fear assail your relationship, as they threaten all relationships at one time or another, remember to focus on what is right between you, not only the part which seems wrong. In this way, you can ride out the storms when clouds hide the face of the sun in your lives—remembering that even if you lose sight of it for a moment, the sun is still there. And if each of you takes responsibility for the quality of your life together, it will be marked by abundance and delight.

NATIVE AMERICAN (CHEROKEE)

God in heaven above, please protect the ones we love. We honor all you created as we pledge our hearts and lives together. We honor Mother Earth and ask for our marriage to be abundant and grow stronger through the seasons. We honor fire and ask that our union be warm and glowing with love in our hearts. We honor wind and ask that we sail through life safe and calm as in our father's arms. We honor water to clean and soothe our relationship—that it may never thirst for love. With all the forces of the universe you created, we pray for harmony as we grow forever young together. Amen.

PRESBYTERIAN

I, ____, take you to be my wedded wife/husband, and I do promise before God and these witnesses to be your loving and faithful wife/husband, in plenty and in want, in joy and in sorrow, in sickness and in health, as long as we both shall live.

PROTESTANT

Please note that many Protestant denominations, including Lutheran, Methodist, Episcopalian, Presbyterian, and some Baptist houses of worship, may revolve their set vows upon a model similar to *The Book of Common Prayers*. That said, you'll find many similar phrases in each of them.

PROTESTANT, NON-DENOMINATIONAL

I, ____, take thee, ____, to be my wedded husband/wife, to have and to hold, from this day forward, for better, for worse, for richer, for poorer, in sickness and in health, to love and to cherish, till death do us part, according to God's holy ordinance: and thereto I pledge thee my faith.

UNITARIAN

Keep in mind that most Unitarian weddings are designed by the ministers performing the service and *not* by a strict code of religious vow by-the-book formatting. That said, here is a model of what you might find as the template for Unitarian vows:

The minister asks the bride and the groom respectively:

_____, will you take _____ to be your husband/wife; love, honor, and cherish him/her now and forevermore?

The bride and groom answer in turn, "I will."

The minister then asks bride and groom to repeat, respectively:

I, _____, take you, _____, to be my husband/wife; to have and to hold from this day forward, for better, for worse, for richer, for poorer, in sickness and in health, to love and cherish always.

QUAKER

In the presence of God and these our Friends, I take thee to be my husband/wife, promising with divine assistance to be unto thee a loving and faithful husband/wife as long as we both shall live.

(Note: In these modern times, many Quaker couples then take the moments after these traditional vows to recite more personalized vows to one another.)

BUDDHIST

In the future, happy occasions will come as surely as the morning. Difficult times will come as surely as the night. When things go joyously, meditate according to the Buddhist tradition. When things go badly, meditate. Meditation in the manner of the Compassionate Buddha will guide your life. To say the words "love" and "compassion" is easy. But to accept that love and compassion are built upon patience and perseverance is not easy.

INTERFAITH WEDDINGS

Interfaith ceremonies offer the opportunity to blend the best of both worlds, either having two separate religious vow ceremonies, each led by officiants from both faiths, or truly personalizing the vow combination by expertly weaving the traditions, rituals, and words of both vow ceremonies together, according to the guidance of your officiants.

In chapter 13, from pages 98-105, several interfaith officiants share with you their sample vows, including vows they've written with the couples they married. Flip ahead to that section in order to explore several personalized, heartfelt vows and vow responses in the realm of interfaith and secular weddings.

2

Traditional Poetry and Readings

For a bit of inspiration from some of the most poetic, visionary, and romantic writers in history, I've listed just a small sampling of well known sonnets, poems, and writings you might wish to incorporate into your vows. Perhaps you'll quote the Bard directly. Perhaps you'll take some creative freedom and adapt the wording from "you" to "I" or "we," in order to make lyrical sense as you profess these words to your bride or groom. Take a few lines, or take the entire reading if you so choose.

You might take a quote, such as Helen Keller's "Life is either a daring adventure or nothing at all," and then talk about how your beloved has brought such adventure and excitement to your life, brought *you* more to life, and how you look forward to your future adventures together. It's just this kind of expanding on readings that allows you to tailor any sentiments to your own partnership.

The choices are yours, and I encourage you to see this list merely as a jumping-off point. Take the time to explore the universe of love poetry, sonnets, scriptures, and haiku out in the printed world. Research the Internet to find obscure love poetry, set up camp in a library or charming old book store and read for further illumination.

For centuries, great lovers before you have spoken words of love and commitment; some have immortalized them in their collected works, and all would gladly lend you their way with words so that you might express your heart's true feelings on your wedding day.

POETRY

Sonnet 43

by Elizabeth Barrett Browning

How do I love thee? Let me count the ways.
I love thee to the depth and breadth and height
My soul can reach, when feeling out of sight
For the ends of Being and ideal Grace.
I love thee to the level of every day's
Most quiet need, by sun and candle-light.
I love thee freely, as men strive for Right;
I love thee purely, as they turn from Praise.
I love thee with the passion put to use
In my old griefs, and with my childhood's faith.
I love thee with a love I seemed to lose
With my lost saints—I love thee with the breath,
Smiles, tears, of all my life!—and, if God choose,
I shall but love thee better after death.

Sonnet 18

by William Shakespeare

Shall I compare thee to a summer's day?

Thou art more lovely and more temperate:
Rough winds do shake the darling buds of May,
And summer's lease hath all too short a date;
Sometime too hot the eye of heaven shines,
And often is his gold complexion dimmed;
And every fair from fair sometime declines,
By chance or nature's changing course untrimmed;
But thy eternal summer shall not fade,
Nor lose possession of that fair thou ow'st;
Nor shall death brag thou wander'st in his shade
Which in eternal lines to time thou grow'st
So long as men can breathe or eyes can see,
So long lives this, and this gives life to thee.

From *As You Like It*
by William Shakespeare
Who ever lov'd that lov'd not at first sight?

From *Romeo and Juliet*
by William Shakespeare
Did my heart love till now? forswear it, sight!
For I ne'er saw true beauty till this night.

From *Romeo and Juliet*
by William Shakespeare
My bounty is as boundless as the sea,
My love as deep:
The more I give to thee,
The more I have,
For both are infinite.

From *Twelfth Night*
by William Shakespeare
Love sought is good, but giv'n unsought, is better.

From *As You Like It*
by William Shakespeare
Phebe: Good shepherd, tell this youth what 'tis to love.

Silvius: It is to be all made of sighs and tears...It is to be all made of faith and service...It is to be all made of fantasy.

All made of passion, and all made of wishes;

All adoration, duty, and observance;

All humbleness, all patience, and impatience;

All purity, all trial, all obeisance.

From *The Two Gentlemen of Verona*
by William Shakespeare
Love can feed on the air.

From *Measure for Measure*
by William Shakespeare
What's mine is yours, and what is yours is mine.

To His Wife Mary
by William Wordsworth
Every day every hour every moment makes me feel more deeply how blessed we are in each other, how purely how faithfully how ardently, and how tenderly we love each other; I put this last word last because, though I am persuaded that a deep affection is not uncommon in married life, yet I am confident that a lively, gushing, thought-employing, spirit-stirring, passion of love is very rare even among good people...O Mary I love you with a passion of love which grows 'til I tremble to think of its strength.

Love
by Christina Rossetti
What is the beginning? Love.

What is the course? Love still.
What is the goal? The goal is love.
On a happy hill.
Is there nothing then but love?
Search we sky or earth
There is nothing out of Love
Hath perpetual worth:
All things flag but only Love,
All things flail and flee;
There is nothing left but Love
Worthy you and me.

From *The Prophet*
by Kahlil Gibran
Love has no other desire but to fulfill itself.

From *The Strength to Love*
by Martin Luther King, Jr.
The meaning of love is not to be confused with some sentimental outpouring. Love is something much more than
emotional bosh...An overflowing love which seeks nothing
in return is the love of God operating in the human
heart...Love is the most durable power in the world. This
creative force, so beautifully exemplified in the life of our
Christ, is the most potent instrument available in mankind's
quest for peace and security...The great military leaders of
the past have gone, and their empires have crumbled and
burned to ashes. But the empire of Jesus, built solidly and
majestically on the foundation of love, is still growing.

From *Letters to a Young Poet*
by Rainer Maria Rilke
For one human being to love another: this is perhaps the

most difficult of all our tasks, the ultimate, the final test and proof, the work for which all other work is only preparation...At first, loving does not mean merging, surrendering, and uniting with another...it is a high inducement to the individual to ripen, to become something in himself, to become world, to become world for himself for another's sake, it is a great, demanding claim upon him, something that chooses him and calls him to vast things.

From *Jane Eyre*
by Charlotte Brontë

> I have for the first time found what I can truly love—I have
>   found you.
> You are my sympathy—my better self—
> My good angel—
> I am bound to you with a strong attachment.
> I think you good, gifted, lovely;
> A fervent, solemn passion is conceived in my heart;
> It leans to you, draws you to my centre and spring of life;
> It wraps my existence around you—
> And kindling in pure, powerful flame,
> Fuses you and me in one.

From *Wuthering Heights*
by Emily Brontë

> ...He's more myself than I am.
> Whatever our souls are made of, his and mine are the same...
> If all else perished and he remained,
> I should still continue to be,
> And if all else remained and he were annihilated,
> The universe would turn to a might stranger...
> He's always, always on my mind;
> Not as pleasure to myself,
> But as my own being.

From *A Navajo Wedding Ceremony*
(Many couples are adapting this writing to read "we" and "us" instead of "you" to reflect the words as vows between the couple. It's often made a part of the unity candle ritual, if not a part of the actual vows.)

Now you have lit a fire and that fire should not go out. The two of you now have a fire that represents love, understanding and a philosophy of life. It will give you heat, food, warmth and happiness. The new fire represents a new beginning—a new life and a new family. The fire should keep burning; you should stay together. You have lit the fire for life, until old age separates you.

RELIGIOUS READINGS (ALL VERSES FROM THE REVISED STANDARD VERSION)

If I speak in the tongues of men and of angels, but have not love, I am a noisy gong or a clanging cymbal. And if I have prophetic powers, and understand all mysteries and all knowledge, and if I have all faith, so as to remove mountains, but have not love, I am nothing. If I give away all I have, and if I deliver my body to be burned, but have not love, I gain nothing. Love is patient and kind; love is not jealous or boastful; it is not arrogant or rude. Love does not insist on its own way; it is not irritable or resentful; it does not rejoice at wrong, but rejoices in the right. Love bears all things, believes all things, hopes all things, endures all things. Love never ends; as for prophecies, they will pass away; as for tongues, they will cease; as for knowledge, it will pass away. For our knowledge is imperfect and our prophecy is imperfect; but when the perfect comes, the imperfect will pass away. When I was a child, I spoke like a child, I thought like a child, I reasoned like a child; when I became a man, I gave up childish ways. For now we see in a mirror dimly [in some translations "as through a glass darkly"], but then face to face. Now I know in part; then I shall understand fully, even as I have been fully understood. So faith, hope, love abide, these three; but the greatest of these is love.

—I Corinthians 13:1-13

I have found the one whom my soul loves.

—Song of Solomon 3:4

There is no fear in love, but perfect love casts out fear.

—I John 4:18

Let us not love in word or speech; but in deed and in truth.

—I John 3:18

Husbands should love their wives as their own bodies.
He who loves his wife loves himself.

—Ephesians 5:28

QUOTES
I came alive when I started loving you.

—C.S. Lewis

To love someone is to see a miracle invisible to others.

—Francois Mauriac

The journey is always towards the other soul.

—D.H. Lawrence

Where there is love, there is life.

—Mahatma Gandhi

In dreams and in love, there are no impossibilities.

—Janos Arany

When two people are at one in their inmost hearts,
they shatter even the strength of iron or of bronze.

—*I Ching*

Those alone are wise who know how to love.

—Seneca

If you would marry wisely, marry your equal.

—Ovid

The moment you have in your heart this extraordinary thing
called love and feel the depth, the delight, the ecstasy of it,
you will discover that for you the world is transformed.

—Jiddu Krishnamurti

I am, in every thought of my heart, yours.

—Woodrow Wilson

The only true gift is a portion of yourself.

—Ralph Waldo Emerson

When one has once fully entered the realm of love, the
world—no matter how imperfect—becomes rich and beautiful, for it consists solely of opportunities for love.

—Soren Kierkegaard

Love is friendship set on fire.

—Jeremy Taylor

Love indeed is a light from heaven, a spark of that immortal
fire.

—Lord Byron

Deeper than speech our love,
Stronger than life our tether.

—Rudyard Kipling

The best and most beautiful things in the world cannot be
seen or even touched. They must be felt with the heart.

—Helen Keller

Life is either a daring adventure or nothing at all.

—Helen Keller

Dreams are necessary to life.

—Anais Nin

Love is life. If you miss love, you miss life.

—Leo Buscaglia

Never above you.
Never below you.
Always beside you.

—Walter Winchell

The most precious possession that ever comes to a man in
this world is a woman's heart.

—J.G. Holland

The best proof of love is trust.

—Dr. Joyce Brothers

Love is the master key that opens the gates to happiness.

—Oliver Wendell Holmes

Love is, above all, the gift of oneself.

—Jean Anouilh

Love is the wine of existence.

—Henry Ward Beecher

Love reflects the thing beloved.

—Alfred Tennyson

Whoever said love is blind is dead wrong. Love is the only thing that lets us see each other with the remotest accuracy.

—Martha Beck

Love has made its best interpreter a sigh.

—Lord Byron

Words of love are works of love.

—W.R. Alger

We loved with a love that was more than a love.

—Edgar Allan Poe, "Annabel Lee"

They do not love, that do not show their love.

—William Shakespeare, *Two Gentlemen of Verona*

Love and desire are the spirit's wings to great deeds.

—Goethe

Love has no age. It is always young.

—Blaise Pascal

It is love that asks, that seeks, that knocks, that finds, and is faithful to what it finds.

—St. Augustine

The motto of chivalry is also the motto of wisdom; to serve all and love but one.

—Balzac

The supreme happiness in life is the assurance of being loved; of being loved for oneself, even in spite of oneself.

—Victor Hugo, *Les Misérables*

Follow your bliss, and doors will open where there were no doors before.

–Joseph Campbell

Love is always bestowed as a gift —freely, willingly and without expectation.

–Leo Buscaglia

Part Two:

Making It Your Own

3

Appreciation

In order to make your vows truly personalized, they have to be *personal*. And that means talking about the one you love. What does he bring to your life? What do you love about him? What makes him the most special person in your world? What makes him so perfect for you, and you so perfect *with* him?

No pre-written vow wording could ever capture the traits of each of you as individuals and of the couple you make together. So take some time right now to search your heart and put that indescribable feeling you get from him into *words*, to explore and pinpoint exactly what it is that makes you love him. And then you get to infuse your wedding vows with a genuine depth of appreciation that's one of a kind.

Let's get started with the following list of examples.

WHAT I APPRECIATE ABOUT YOU...
The way you make me laugh
Your patience
Your kindness to me and to others
Your willingness to go along with my spontaneous plans
Your fabulous cooking

How you make every day one to remember

How you can be tough one minute and tender the next

That romantic side of you that warms my heart

That you always side with me

That you and I take turns being the voice of reason

How you make me feel appreciated

How passionate you get when you really believe in something

That you share your passions with me

The way you look at me over breakfast

That you make our love a priority in your life

The wonderful sound of your key in the lock at the end of the day

The charge I get from just one kiss from you

The little things you do to let me know you're thinking of me

That you don't let me take myself or anything else too seriously

How fully you love those you care about

Now, it's your turn...

*

*

*

WHAT YOU BRING TO MY LIFE...

A warm place to come home to

The safety of our friendship and love together

Laughter

New adventures to enjoy together

Inspiration

Blessings beyond belief
A warm heart to call my own
A new reason to be a better person every day
Proof that true love still exists
I still get butterflies in my stomach when I look at you
A renewed spirit
Humility when I need it, honor when I deserve it,
    and humor all the time
The freedom to fly and always to come home to you
A soaring sense of joy
A place of belonging
Faith that *all* things are possible
The ability to dream bigger dreams
Blue morning skies and starry nights
Pure satisfaction
Utter bliss
Now it's your turn:
*
*
*

WHAT I SEE IN OUR FUTURE TOGETHER
I see us…
Building a home together
Welcoming children in our lives
Naming our children together
Being a terrific team
Inspiring others with our partnership
Old and gray, walking hand in hand along the beach
Sitting on our porch at sunset with a glass of wine,

holding hands

Always dancing to our song

Dreaming new dreams and making them come true

Loved by one another, and by all we those love, forever

Walking off into the sunset together

Exploring the world together

Learning and growing together

Facing all of life's challenges together

Loving every new wrinkle on each other's faces

Lifting each other to new heights of happiness

Sharing our faith with those we love

Having your face as the last thing I see each night

Seeing your face on the pillow next to me first thing each morning

Sunday mornings in bed with the newspaper and the dogs at our feet

Growing more in love each day

Now it's your turn:

*

*

*

WHAT OUR MARRIAGE MEANS TO ME

That I am finally yours

That we are finally a "we"

That we will spend our lives making each other happy

That we can finally begin making our dreams come true

That we will be a family united forever

That your family is my family, and mine is yours

That dreams do come true

That I must have done something good along the way

That my heart is full

That I have been blessed beyond belief

That Someone heard my prayers

That love is worth waiting for

Now it's your turn:

*

*

*

I AM LUCKY TO HAVE YOU BECAUSE...

I always dreamed of meeting the one perfect person
for me

You make it so easy to love you

In all my life, I have never been so in love

You give from your heart, with no end in sight

You're the kindest, most generous person I know

You treat me the way I always hoped to be treated

You've never stopped romancing me

You only get better and better with time

You surprise me with things I never even knew I
wanted

You make life so much fun

You want so much for us in the future

They don't make them like you anymore...

Now it's your turn:

*

*

*

4

Promises to Make and Keep

In this section, you'll consider a collection of promises you might wish to make to each other within your vows. Choose carefully, and speak from your heart, as these words will make the foundation of your marriage stronger:

I PROMISE TO...
Love you
Honor you
Cherish you
Adore you
Be faithful to you
Be loyal to you
Be open and honest with you
Be your best friend and companion
Be your partner
Be your lover
Be your confidant(e)
Be your strongest supporter
Be kind to you
Live with you
Laugh with you
Dream with you

Bring our dreams to life

Help you bring your dreams to life

Build a warm and loving home with you

Build a family with you

Be your safe place to rest

Take turns leading and following

Care for you, and be cared for by you

Hold you up with respect

Learn from you

Open my heart to yours

Welcome miracles in our lives

Make our marriage my top priority

Make you my top priority

Make our family my top priority

Hold tight when the going gets rough

Never give up on us, you, or myself

Meet each challenge life brings, right by your side

Celebrate the good times

Comfort you through the bad times

Keep renewing our friendship and our relationship

Carry you when you are weak

Allow you to carry me when I am weak

Always remind you of the good I see in you

Always find new ways to show you how much I love you

Express my gratitude

Earn your love every day

Keep close to you, even when we are far away

Always take the time to look at the stars

Walk with you wherever the path might lead us

Sail off with you and chase every sunset together

Fall in love with you over and over, and over again
Always remember the first stirrings of our love
Always kiss you goodnight
Accomplish more together than either of us could
  alone
Surpass our wildest dreams
Always be there when you reach for me
Share this adventure of a lifetime with you
Make each new day more exciting than the last
Allow you your bad moods and love you anyway
Love you for your quirks, as well as your shining traits
Agree when necessary, compromise when necessary
Respect your opinion *and* allow different opinions
Bring my best self to this marriage
Bring you peace and serenity when you need it
Turn away from temptations and interference
Listen to you, and at the same time, hear you
Draw on my own strengths to bring out yours
Calm your fears
Be your shoulder to cry on
Protect you from harm
Come to your rescue
Embrace your family
Embrace your children
Forgive you
Show you compassion
Remember that we are both only human
Give 100 percent of myself to you
Spend the rest of my life with you
Always have faith in you

Always believe in you
Grow old along with you
Love you without reservation
Allow our love to cast out all fear
Seek your wisdom and insight and share my own
 with you
Now it's your turn...
*
*
*

I PROMISE TO ALWAYS BE YOURS...
In good times and in bad
In sickness and in health
In happiness and sadness
In your triumphs and defeats
For richer for poorer
In plenty and in want
When we are near or far from one another
When our path takes unexpected turns
When life challenges us
When life rewards us
As the seasons change
When we question ourselves and each other
No matter the circumstances

AND IN CLOSING, I PROMISE TO...
Keep these vows sacred forever
Keep these vows close to my heart
Live these vows forever

5

Theme Vows

Build your vows on a theme, and you'll bring brighter life to your words. If your thoughts are swirling and you can't find a place to start, think of the one theme that applies to your relationship with your intended. It could be "friendship" if he's your best friend above all. It could be "faith" if you both share a deep commitment to your religious beliefs. I've supplied some samples in this chapter, along with original writings and classic quotes to draw from.

LOVE AT FIRST SIGHT
The face of all the world is changed, I think,
Since I first heard the footsteps of thy soul.
                                        —Elizabeth Barrett Browning

This was love at first sight, love everlasting:
a feeling unknown, unhoped for, unexpected—
in so far as it could be a matter of conscious awareness;
it took entire possession of him, and he understood,
with joyous amazement,
that this was for life.

                                        —Thomas Mann

Love makes your soul crawl out from its hiding place.
                                        —Zora Neale Hurston

From *She Was a Phantom Of Delight*
by William Wordsworth

> She was a Phantom of delight
> When first she gleamed upon my sight;
> A lovely Apparition, sent
> To be a moment's ornament;
> Her eyes as stars of Twilight fair,
> Like Twilight's, too, her dusky hair;
> But all things else about her drawn
> From May-time and the cheerful Dawn.

> When I first saw you, I knew.
> I knew you were the one for me,
> That my life had just taken a big step forward.
> It took me a while to catch my breath
> And to realize the enormity of what changed,
> What clicked inside me,
> When I first saw you, first spoke to you, first
>   held your hand,
> First kissed you.
> It was love at first sight, and then love at *every*
>   sight of you.

> They say that love at first sight is a myth,
> something made up for storybooks and movies
> and songs.
> I used to believe that,
> Until I saw you.
> When you walked into my life,
> All the cynicism I'd come to know
> Just melted away.

And I believed in True Love,
I believed that dreams come true.
I believed that there is one person on this
    earth meant for each one of us.
That's what love does,
And that's what you did for me the moment
    I first saw you.
You made me believe in love
Enough to run toward it...
To run toward you.

I remember the first time I saw you...
You had just come in from the rain,
Your hair was all wet, and you were tugging
    at your jacket
Trying to look okay for our first date.
Even soaked, you were beautiful to me,
And I fell in love with you on the spot.
Without a word...
Just from that look in your big brown eyes,
Because you *smiled*.

FRIENDSHIP

My fellow, my companion, held most dear.
My soul, my other self,
My inward friend.

—Mary Sidney Herbert

...Friends do not live in harmony, merely, as some say, but in melody.

—Henry David Thoreau

Friends…
They cherish each other's hopes.
They are kind to each other's dreams.

—Henry David Thoreau

One of the most beautiful qualities of true friendship is to understand and be understood.

—Seneca

The glory of friendship is not the outstretched hand, nor the kindly smile nor the joy of companionship; it is the spiritual inspiration that comes to one when he discovers that someone else believes in him and is willing to trust him.

—Ralph Waldo Emerson

Blessed is the influence of one true, loving human soul on another.

—George Eliot

My best friend is one who brings out the best in me.

—Henry Ford

Continue to be my friend, as you will always find me yours.

—Ludwig van Beethoven

A friend knows the song in my heart and sings it to me when my memory fails.

—Donna Roberts

Lots of people want to ride with you in the limo, but what you want is someone who will take the bus with you when the limo breaks down.

—Oprah Winfrey

I value the friend who for me finds time on his calendar, but I cherish the friend who does not consult his calendar.

—Robert Brault

I always felt that the great high privilege, relief and comfort of friends was that one had to explain nothing.

—Katherine Mansfield

My fair one, let us swear an eternal friendship.

—Jean Baptiste Moliere

Each friend represents a world in us, a world possibly not born until they arrive, and it is only by this meeting that a new world is born.

—Anaïs Nin

_____, you are my best friend.
I stand here with you now to join our lives in
    marriage,
To love each other as husband and wife
And to adore each other as True Friends.

You are my forever friend,
and I am yours.
Love can only live between equals,
Between friends.
So I offer my love to you,
I offer my heart to you,
And I promise always to be your faithful
    friend and wife/husband.
Forever.

FAITH

I never knew how to worship until I knew how to love.
— Henry Ward Beecher

As we become purer channels for God's light, we develop an appetite for the sweetness that is possible in this world. A miracle worker is not geared toward fighting the world that is, but toward creating the world that could be.
— Marianne Williamson

If I choose to bless another person, I will always end up feeling more blessed.
— Marianne Williamson

A hero is someone who has given his or her life to something bigger than oneself.
— Joseph Campbell

I'm working my way toward divinity.
— Bette Midler

Thee lift me, and I'll lift thee, and we'll ascend together.
— Quaker proverb

> ____, the Father above brought us together,
> As part of some wonderful divine plan for our lives.
> We were made for one another, in His name,
> To fulfill His wishes,
> And to create a fruitful life together.
> I promise you my heart,
> With all faith that we are meant to be together.

We will love one another as God loves us.
Unconditionally, in our best moments and
    worst.
We will always have faith in one another
And love for one another,
For as long as we both shall live.

BEAUTY

If either man or woman would realize the full power of
personal beauty, it must be by cherishing noble thoughts and
hopes and purposes; by having something to do and something to live for that is worthy of humanity.

—Rose Kennedy

Sexiness wears thin after a while and beauty fades. But to be
married to a man who makes you laugh every day, ah, now
that is a real treat.

—Joanne Woodward

The best smell in the world is the man that you love.

—Jennifer Aniston

O, thou art fairer than the evening air
Clad in the beauty of a thousand stars.

—Christopher Marlowe, *Faustus*

Love is a great beautifier.

—Louisa May Alcott, *Little Women*

You don't love a woman because she is beautiful,
but she is beautiful because you love her.

—Anonymous

A thing of beauty is a joy for ever.

—John Keats, "Endymion"

_____, you're so beautiful to me.
I can hardly believe how stunning you are,
How your beauty from within just pours out
    and warms me,
And how you make each day more beautiful
    than the last
Just by being a part of it.

You're almost too beautiful right now,
and I can't take my eyes off you.
And this I promise…
Never to take my eyes off you,
Never to take my eyes away from our part-
    nership,
And to make each day as beautiful for you
As you are to me.

PARTNERSHIP

What greater thing is there for two human souls than to feel
that they are joined together
To strengthen each other in all labours,
To minister to each other in all sorrow,
To share with each other in all gladness,
To be one with each other in the silent, unspoken memories?
—George Eliot

…She gets into the remotest recesses of my heart, and shines
all through me.

—Nathaniel Hawthorne

You cannot be lonely if you like the person you're alone with.
—Dr. Wayne W. Dyer

Remember we all stumble, every one of us. That's why it's a comfort to go hand in hand.

—Emily Kimbrough

Affection is responsible for nine-tenths of whatever solid and durable happiness there is in our lives.

—C.S. Lewis

Aim at heaven, and you will get earth thrown in. Aim at earth, and you will get neither.

—C.S. Lewis

Long after moments of closeness have passed,
A part of you remains with me
And warms the places your hands have touched
And hastens my heart for your return.

—Robert Sexton

In loving, you lean on someone to hold them up.

—Rod McKuen

Whatever our souls are made of, his and mine are the same.

—Emily Brontë

To bear each other's burdens, never to ask each other for anything inconsistent with virtue and rectitude, and not only to serve and to love, but also to respect each other...

—Cicero

What do we live for, if it is not to make life less difficult to each other?

—George Eliot, *Middlemarch*

I couldn't ask for a more perfect partner
to share the joys and challenges of my life.
We're so perfectly paired,

So evenly matched,
So complementary to one another.
I vow always to love you as my partner in life,
My partner in love,
And my partner in the workings of every day
   and night that we have together.

Take my hand today and always,
and let's share a beautiful life
and a beautiful love
As equals and allies
In this challenging and rewarding world,
To see what we can build together.

What Marriage Is

Love is not getting, but giving.
It is goodness and honor and peace and pure living.
—Henry Van Dyke

From *The Clod and the Pebble*
by William Blake
   Love seeketh not itself to please,
   Nor for itself hath any care,
   But for another gives its ease,
   And builds a heaven in hell's despair.

We've got this gift of love, but love is like a precious plant.
You can't just accept it and leave it in the cupboard or just
think it's going to get on by itself. You've got to keep water-
ing it. You've got to really look after it and nurture it.
—John Lennon

Imagination is the highest kite that one can fly.

—Lauren Bacall

It's the sweet, simple things of life which are the real ones after all.

—Laura Ingalls Wilder

He has achieved success who has lived well, laughed often, and loved much.

—Betty Anderson Stanley

The first duty of love is to listen.

—Paul Tillich

Let us always meet each other with a smile, for a smile is the beginning of love.

—Mother Teresa

Chains do not hold a marriage together. It is threads, hundreds of tiny threads which sew people together through the years.

—Simone Signoret

Love does not consist of gazing at each other but in looking together in the same direction.

—Antoine de Saint-Exupéry

A goal is a dream that has an ending.

—Duke Ellington

Joy is not in things.
It is in us.

—Richard Wagner

What I need is someone who will make me do what I can.

—Ralph Waldo Emerson

Two persons cannot long be friends, if they cannot forgive each other's little failings.

—Jean de la Bruyere

_____, I take you to be my husband.
I join with you in marriage
So that we may build the same kind of happy
    and fulfilled life together
As my parents have, as your parents have,
As our grandparents have before us.
It is my dream, my wish, and my promise to
    you now
That we will enjoy the blessings of a life well
    lived together
And that we will be as happy as the happiest
    couples we know.

We know what makes a marriage work.
Love, commitment, communication,
Laughter, support, honesty,
Valuing one another above all others.
I promise these and so much more to you
    now.
I promise to hold our marriage up as a
    treasured gift,
To give you my all
Every day,
And to be your loving partner forever.

6

May I Quote You? Lyrics of Love from Your Favorite Songs

Musicians and composers make millions of dollars putting thoughts, promises, and expressions of love into song, so why not borrow some of their famous words for your vows? You could use part of the lyrics from the song that will be your First Dance. Or you could use the words from the first song you ever slow-danced to, the song that played the night you got engaged, the song that always reminds you of each other. Music carries our memories, so make the memories go even deeper by weaving them into your vows.

I've collected some of the most popular love songs ever written and ever played at the most romantic weddings. Now, you can "sample" their lyrics. Even better than striking a sentimental chord with your new spouse (and with your guests), you'll think of your wedding vows whenever you hear that song on the radio.

A quick word before you start quoting Paul McCartney or Sarah McLachlan...keep your lyric lifts *short*. Only use one or two lines. Anything more than that is a dead giveaway that you couldn't come up with anything on your own!

THE SONGS AND PERFORMING ARTISTS

"A Kiss to Build a Dream On"—Louis Armstrong

"A Whole New World (Aladdin's Theme)"—Peabo Bryson

"All I Ask of You"—Michael Crawford

"All My Life"—Aaron Neville and Linda Ronstadt

"All the Things You Are"—Ella Fitzgerald

"All the Way"—Frank Sinatra

"Amazed"—Lonestar

"As Time Goes By"—Jimmy Durante

"At Last"—Etta James (my favorite!)

"A Wink And A Smile"—Harry Connick, Jr.

"Beautiful In My Eyes"—Joshua Kadison

"Because You Loved Me"—Celine Dion

"Be My Life's Companion"—Louis Armstrong

"Best Thing That Ever Happened to Me"—Gladys Knight

"Breathe"—Faith Hill

"Can You Feel The Love Tonight?"—Elton John

"Can't Help Falling In Love"—Elvis Presley

"Can't Take My Eyes Off You"—Frankie Valli

"Chances Are"—Johnny Mathis

"Come Away With Me"—Norah Jones

"Come Rain Or Come Shine"—Billie Holiday

"Come What May"—Ewan McGregor and Nicole Kidman

"Could Not Ask for More"—Edwin McCain

"(Everything I Do) I Do It For You"—Bryan Adams

"Faithfully"—Journey

"Fly Me to the Moon"—Frank Sinatra

"From This Moment On"—Shania Twain

"Have I Told You Lately"—Rod Stewart/Van Morrison

"I Can't Give You Anything But Love"—Louis Armstrong

"Ice Cream"—Sarah McLachlan

"I Cross my Heart"—George Strait

"In My Life"—The Beatles

"In Your Eyes"—Peter Gabriel

"I Only Have Eyes For You"—Art Garfunkel

"It Had To Be You"—Harry Connick, Jr.

"Just The Way You Are"—Billy Joel

"Let It Be Me"—Nina Simone

"Longer"—Dan Fogelberg

"Love Is Here To Stay"—Harry Connick, Jr.

"Make Someone Happy"—Jimmy Durante

"Maybe I'm Amazed"—Paul McCartney

"More"—Bobby Darin

"My Baby Just Cares For Me"—Nina Simone

"My Love Is Your Love"—Whitney Houston

"My Romance"—Carly Simon

"Nobody Does It Better"—Carly Simon

"Only You"—The Platters

"Save The Best For Last"—Vanessa Williams

"Sea of Love"—The Honeydrippers

"She's Got a Way"—Billy Joel

"Stand by Me"—Ben E. King

"That's All"—Sam Harris

"The Best Is Yet To Come"—Frank Sinatra

"The Way You Look Tonight"—Frank Sinatra

"The Way You Love Me"—Faith Hill

"Time In A Bottle"—Jim Croce

"To Make You Feel My Love"—Garth Brooks

"True Companion"—Marc Cohn

"True Love"—Elton John

"Twelfth Of Never"—Johnny Mathis

"Unforgettable"—Nat King Cole

"Up Where We Belong"—Joe Cocker and Jennifer Warnes

"Vision Of Love"—Mariah Carey

"We Are In Love"—Harry Connick, Jr.

"What a Wonderful World"—Louis Armstrong

"When I Am With You"—Johnny Mathis (Look this one up! It's amazing!)

"When I Fall In Love"—Celine Dion and Clive Griffin

"Wonderful Tonight"—Eric Clapton

"You and I"—Eddie Rabbitt and Crystal Gayle

"You Are So Beautiful"—Joe Cocker

"You Are the Sunshine of My Life"—Stevie Wonder

"You Go To My Head"—Rod Stewart

"You'll Never Walk Alone"—Aretha Franklin

"You're Getting to Be a Habit With Me"—Frank Sinatra

"Your Song"—Ewan McGregor and Nicole Kidman

"You Send Me"—Sam Cooke

Part Three:

Vows for Specialty Weddings

7

Vows for Couples with Kids

If one or both of you have children from previous relationships, it's a wise and wonderful idea to add a separate statement of promise and love to your children after your couple's marriage vows. With the words you say, you can make this moment within the ceremony even more special by presenting the child (or children) with a very special gift just for them—perhaps a diamond pendant, a heart locket, a birthstone ring, or a family medallion.

Your vow might be a simple script such as the following:

You say:

____, I take you to be my son/daughter. I promise to always love you and support you, to hold you close and watch over you forever and always.

The child will then repeat similar vows:

I, ____, take you, ____, to be my mother/father/Mom/Dad. I promise to love you and honor you forever and always.

For sanity's sake and because small children might get shy when asked to speak in the spotlight, most couples keep the children's portion of the vows very brief and very simple.

For additional ideas on vows you can devote to children of all ages, read on:

_____, as I promise my love, support, and loyalty to your mother/father, I also offer the same to you. From the moment I stepped into your lives, the warmth and caring I see your mother/father give you has made me so happy, and your presence in my life makes this union that much more precious to me. I promise to be there for you when you need me, to support you in all that you do, to give you a warm and comfortable home, and I look forward to adding something special to your life for all the days to come. I adore you, I appreciate you, and I thank you for being the wonderful child that you are.

The groom says:

_____, they say the best thing a man can do for a child is to love his mother well. I promise to carry out that promise for her happiness and for yours. I am so proud of the person you are, of everything you do, and I promise to always stand by you in the future. Thank you for letting me into your life, for opening up to me, and for welcoming me into the family that

you've always known. I promise with everything
I am to always make you a top priority, to guide
you, to laugh with you and make you laugh, to
dry your tears, and to watch proudly as you
continue to impress us both.

With the presentation of necklace, locket, family
medallion, or special gift:
_____, I offer this gift as a token of my prom-
ise to you, that I will always be a loving parent,
and that you will always be assured of my loyalty
and commitment to you.

If it is a necklace, add:
Wear it close to your heart as a reminder of
how I've taken you into *my* heart as my own
beloved daughter.

If it is a locket, add:
As this heart opens to hold your own heart's
desire, know that my heart is full of gratitude
for the love that you give me every day.

If it is a diamond, add:
This stone may be precious to some, but no
stone, no gem, no treasure on earth is more
precious to me than you are.

If it is a family medallion, add:
This medallion is a symbol of intertwined

circles, one each for you, for your parents, and for the life that we'll build together. As I give this to you, I want you to always remember that the three circles also represent my faith, hope, and love for you as my own child.

If it is a ring, add:

A ring is a circle, unending, symbolizing eternity. Like our wedding rings, this ring I give to you is a symbol of my promise to love you, support you, guide you, and believe in you forever and ever.

Vow for Infants

_____, there are no words to express how blessed I am at this moment. To hold you in my arms and call you my son/daughter is a gift I'm both humbled and thrilled by. I promise to love you with all of my heart, to guide you, to comfort you, and to watch you develop into the wonderful person you're soon to become. You're our angel, and I love you.

Vow Responses for Children

Remember to tailor your child's participation level according to: age, readiness for speaking at such a high-pressure moment, personality strengths, and shyness level.

Vows written by older children are greatly appreciated by parents, because it means so much more that the child created them from his/her own sentiments and not from a script either parent might have written. This is a wonderful gift from child to parents, and I encourage you to invite your child or children to join in.

Here are some suggestions for kid-friendly vow responses:

I take you, ____, to be my mother/father, forever and always.

I take you, ____, to be my mother/father; to look up to you always, to listen to you, and to laugh with you. I promise to love you always, and to always remember that you love me.

For Older Children:

I, ____, take you, ____, to be my mother/father, to love you, honor you, and respect you always, to bring you the best that I can be, and to appreciate the best that you can be, as we grow together in our family forever.

I, ____, take you, ____, to be my mother/father, in the best and worst of times, in sickness and in health, while we laugh together, cry together, work together, and play together. Whether we're near or far, you will always be special to me, as a parent that I'm lucky to have.

Borrow From...Children's Books?

That's exactly the horizon opened by Jill Althouse-Wood, creator of www.mortalmom.com. Jill says that children's storybooks are a great place to look for vows that children can relate to and enjoy. Jill's expert advice as a mother, writer, and artist goes on for further inspiration:

"In the movie *Miami Rhapsody*, protagonist Gwyn Marcus has her doubts about marriage even before she attends her sister's wedding. The ceremony doesn't help Gwyn's uncertainty, especially when the sacred vows take on a decidedly 'Seuss'ian twist. The exact words escape me, but they echoed the gentle poetry of *Green Eggs and Ham*, '...and I will love you in the rain, and in the dark and on a train.' While such vows may sound sacrilegious when spoken by bride to groom, the storybook sentiment may be enchanting when repeated *to a five-year-old*. Consider other beloved books, and peruse them for young children's vow ideas.

"*The Runaway Bunny* by Margaret Wise Brown has some delightful quotes. 'If you go flying on a flying trapeze...I will be a tightrope walker and I will walk across the air to you.' or 'If you become a bird and fly away from me...I will be a tree that you come home to.'

"Or ponder a book that I cannot read aloud without crying: *Love You Forever* by Robert Munsch. My son copied some of the lines onto a Mother's Day card he gave me recently. 'I'll love you forever. I'll like you for always. As long as you're living, my Mommy, you'll be.' What new stepmom would not cry to hear those words spoken to her in a wedding ceremony?

"As a final offering, I give you *Guess How Much I Love*

You by Sam McBratney. In this book, a mother rabbit and her baby bunny compete for the biggest declaration of love. A child and parent could recite these words back and forth to one another. 'Guess how much I love you...I love you all the way down the lane as far as the river...I love you across the river and over the hills...I love you right up to the moon...I love you right up to the moon—and back.'

"Children's books come complete with all the charm, the hook, and the poetry. They are prepackaged wedding vows, when you read them looking for promises. If the child already has a large collection of books, take time to go through them together, and find a sentiment you can make your own."

8

Vows for Second Weddings and Wedding Vow Renewals

So many couples marrying for the second, third, even fifth time around wonder, *What am I allowed to do this time around?* The bride who's already taken a previous trip down the aisle wonders if she can wear a white gown. A couple wonders if they can still have a formal, traditional wedding. What are the rules?

The answer is: there *are* no rules. You can wear white, you can have a big, formal white wedding, and you *can* either recite traditional wedding vows or write new ones of your own. Everything is as you wish, since there is no longer any stigma or shame in getting married again. You can plan your wedding now as if you never had one before. You can celebrate big if you want to, and you can write personalized vows that will wow your crowd and bring tears to everyone's eyes.

The beautiful thing about second weddings is that the couple has more of a sense of themselves. They have so much more wisdom this time around, and their vows are very often so much more realistic, so much more sentimental...since they know of what they speak. If this isn't your first trip down the aisle, writing your own vows can be a beautiful thing.

As you plan your wedding, are you subconsciously trying to make *everything* different from the first time around? Some previously-marrieds do just that. They don't want anything to remind them of their past. From the location to the dress to the food to the cake, nothing can be even a slight reminder of their first wedding. For many of these brides and grooms, the vows are where they focus their originality. While they might have recited traditional religious vow script before, this time it's going to be something completely original.

Where are you on this scale? If you don't have a problem with repeating the traditional vows that you've spoken to someone else before, then use or adapt the traditional vows in this book. No Wedding Etiquette Police are going to pop out of the balcony to arrest you. You have complete freedom.

A Woman or a Man with a Past

What do you think about these vows: "The last time I promised to love, honor, and cherish until death do us part, it didn't quite work out that way. But now you're here, and you're so much better than the other guy." Yikes! This may be a pretty extreme example of tacky first-wedding references, but I included it here to illustrate the need for you to consider *how* and *if* you'll make any reference at all to your previous wedding(s).

Again, many second-time brides and grooms go about their wedding plans as if they'd never been married before, so the issue just doesn't come up. But some do wish to acknowledge their histories, particularly if they have children from their first unions. They just do it in a vague, respectful, and proper way—proper towards their ex, and proper towards their new spouse-to-be.

Here are some vow possibilities for the tender and delicate handling of acknowledging your pasts before the Big Day:

> _____, there was a time when I thought
> I would never know a deep and peaceful,
>   full-acceptance love again.
> But then you came along and offered me
>   your heart.
> You restored my faith in true love,
> In chivalry,
> In my own goodness and value,
> In the idea of good things coming to those
>   who wait.
> I stand here before you now to offer you my
>   hand, my heart, and my future.
> I bring you the fruition of my life's experi-
>   ences, the tapestry of my lifetime,
> Just as you bring me yours.
> We are both better people for the lives we've
>   lived to this point,
> For the challenges and struggles we've over-
>   come,

And for the joys we've experienced along the
　　way.
Good things *do* come to those who wait,
And you are all good things to me.
I promise you my undying affection,
　　respect, support, and admiration.
I promise you that I will lift you up as you
　　have lifted me,
And that we will stand in the sunlight
　　together forever.

＿＿＿, I give you my heart and soul
That have been expanded and brightened by
　　your presence in my life,
By your love and laughter,
By the touch of your hand and the smile in
　　your eyes.
I give you all of who I am, and all that I have
　　been,
Everything I've learned in my lifetime,
And the hope I have for our future together.
I promise to love you always,
As I am so proud to call myself your wife.

＿＿＿, you bring me such joy.
I've lived many chapters of a lifetime,
Some happy, some sad, some dramatic, and
　　some forgettable.
And now, as I stand at the start of a new page
　　in my life,

The book becomes *ours.*
The pages leading up to this moment
Have served to make me the woman I am,
The words and storylines and lessons and
    morals all add up to Right Now.
I promise to fill, with you, each page of the
    story of our lives
With goodness, love, and laughter,
With blessings and lessons and the makings
    of our family and home.
The happy ending comes at the *beginning* of
    this storybook life we'll build,
And each page builds upon the previous
    one,
While we love each other until Happily Ever
    After.

When you came along,
you opened windows and doors and hori-
    zons for me,
showing me the world in a new light,
and showing me parts of myself
that I had long forgotten I had tucked away
    for safekeeping.
You brought me to life in a new and won-
    derful way,
Full of light and joy and serenity and excite-
    ment.
I promise, as we join our lives together now,
That I will always be true to you,

And that I will always open windows and
  doors and horizons to you,
Bringing out the best in you,
And bringing out the best in our future
  together.
You have my heart,
Because you earned it.
You valued it and nurtured it,
You gave me your own in the most generous
  way possible.
I will always love and support you,
And I thank you for being my husband/wife.

____, I stand before you
To offer you my hand and my love forever.
There is no Then...
There is only Now...
Our lives have brought us here to this
  moment,
So that we may bring each other happiness
As best friends, as lovers, as confidantes,
As true and equal partners
With full faith and confidence in one
  another.
I love you with all that I am,
I will love and laugh with you forever and
  ever,
And I look only forward to the life we will
  build together.
With this ring, I step towards you in love.

The footsteps we have both left behind us
    have carried us from There to Here,
From friendship to love to marriage,
And they will carry us onward through our
    lives.
I promise always to love you, always to share
    with you,
Always to walk beside you as your faithful
    and loyal husband/wife.

Wedding Vow Renewals

True, it might not be your first time making wedding vows, but you're making them with the same partner! Renewing your wedding vows is a wonderful way to mark the passage of time in a successful marriage, a public declaration that love and partnership do last. Couples who have chosen to renew their vows as a part of their 10th, 20th, 25th, even 50th wedding anniversaries tell me that their words are that much sweeter this time around, with years of friendship and deep love supporting them.

Even better, the family members of these couples, including young adults, comment that it's heartwarming to attend the celebration of a lasting marriage and the renewal of vows. Young people need the example of "how to do it right," and entire families gather together for a fabulous milestone celebration.

If you will be renewing your wedding vows, you can choose from any quotes, readings, or promptings in this book, and you can blend in the theme of lasting love and a renewed bond. Here are some quotes and ideas to consider as you write your own vows:

Young love is a flame:
very pretty, often very hot and fierce,
but still only light and flickering.
The love of the older and disciplined heart
Is as coals: deep, burning, unquenchable.

—Henry Ward Beecher

To me, fair friend, you can never be old
For as you were when first your eye I ey'd,
Such seems your beauty still.

—William Shakespeare, *Sonnet 54*

Love is of immortality.

—Plato, *Symposium*

Love like ours can never die!

—Rudyard Kipling, *The Lovers' Litany*

How vast a memory has love!

—Alexander Pope

Age does not protect you from love. But love, to some extent, protects you from age.

—Anais Nin

To us, family means putting your arms around each other and being there.

—Barbara Bush

I wish to believe in immortality—
I wish to live with you forever.

—John Keats

I took you then for who you were to me,
I take you still for who you are to me,
For what you have brought to my life,
For what you continue to bring,
And for what you will be to me always.
And they said it wouldn't last…

My dearest heart,
You have been my life's blessing,
My greatest gift,
The joy of my days and nights.
Let's join hands once again
And offer one another the peace of our
    company,
The depth of our friendship,
The still-growing horizons of our love.

I offer you my heart today, out loud
And in the company of all the friends and
    family
Who have been with us since our wedding
    day,
And who have come to us and through us
    since.
We are what we are in such great measure
Because of our love for one another,
And because of their love for us.

9

Vows for Destination Weddings

If you are heading to the islands, the beach, the mountains, overseas, or to a resort just an hour from your home, your destination wedding opens up beautiful opportunities to make your wedding vows even more meaningful. Tie them into the beauty and grandeur of your surroundings, or draw from native legend and culture, and you'll create even deeper and more memorable words of a lifetime.

Take, for example, one couple who married in the rainforest overlooking the Seven Sacred Pools in the Haleakala National Park, Hawaii. According to island legend, those natural pools were once the bathing grounds of Hawaiian kings and queens, princesses and princes. The waters were thought to have magical properties, and the footsteps and favor of royalty made the pools an extremely revered site. Choosing the present day pools as the site of their wedding, the couple paid homage to the memory and spirit of those Hawaiian kings and queens—and also enjoyed a moment of royalty themselves as King and Queen of their own wedding day. They did this by dipping their bare toes into the waters while the local officiant recited a Hawaiian wedding blessing with the couples' vows. Their guests loved the cultural tie-in, and the couple loved the unique and culturally respectful enactment of an authentic Hawaiian wedding blessing.

To add a dose of local flavor to your own wedding vows, consider the following:

Have your officiant read a marriage blessing in the native language, and then translate it for your guests. Try your accents out by repeating your vows in the native tongue. With a little practice, and guided by your officiant, you can master a phrase or word easily, giving extra meaning to your ceremony.

Learn the culture. So many tropical islands and international destination cities are ripe with cultural additions that can only add to the loveliness of your wedding vows. In the Caribbean, you might recite your vows as a group of steel drum players provide musical accompaniment to your words. In New Orleans, you can make reference to that city's motto, *Laissez les bon temps rouler* ("Let the good times roll"). In a Scottish castle, you can remark that your groom treats you like a queen. Or grab a cultural symbol and weave it into your ceremony and your vows.

Learn the legends of the area. Your chosen destination might count among its charms many romantic folklore legends of great loves. One couple who married at a rented estate home in Maine were able to reference the story of a sea captain and his wife who lived in that home many years before. Legend has it that they married in the garden, in the very spot where the present couple stood, and lived happily for years as husband and wife. Each year, at sunset on the day of their wedding anniversary, their ghosts can be seen walking hand in hand under the arbors and disappearing into the dunes, loving one another into eternity as they had promised.

Use that gorgeous sunset. A spectacularly setting sun, whether over the ocean or majestic mountains, fills the sky with a veritable light show and makes the waters or leaves dance with ripples of gold. Within your vows, you can mention the symbolism of the setting sun:

> As the sun sets on our lives as single people,
> And as the sky fills with brilliant colors,
> I take you to be my husband.
> I promise to fill your life with brilliant colors
> And give us both the assurance
> That the sun will always rise again on new days
> That we may spend together.

Bask in the beauty of your surroundings. Some outdoor destination weddings are set in fields of flowers, in the gardens of mansions, in arboretums or apple orchards, in mountainous clearings, on scenic overlooks that afford a priceless view of the city skyline in the distance, or on pristine beaches with crashing surf and azure waters for as far as the eye

Coordinate your ceremony for exact sunset time by checking online or in an almanac for the precise sunset time for any location on any day of the year.

can see. Each of these scenes lends an incredible atmosphere to your wedding, and you can use them to make your vows equally unforgettable.

In a wooded glen, reminiscent of Shakespeare's *A Midsummer Night's Dream* or a Jane Austen novel, you can say:

It's wonderful to know that such a beautiful, unspoiled, natural place still exists in this world, and it's wonderful to stand here within it with you, ready to take your hand in our own paradise.

On a sun-kissed beach, you can stand at the water's edge and say:

I will love you as deeply as the ocean, as steadily as the waves, as full of life as the world below the surface, and as refreshingly as a plunge into cool waters on a hot summer day. We'll live a life of adventure, we'll travel the world, and we'll dive into the future starting right here, right now.

Or...

Which is greater? The number of sand grains on this beach, the number of drops of water in the ocean, or the level of my love for you? Today, my love is greater, and tomorrow it will be greater, and the day after even greater than that. Nothing created on earth can be as big, as deep, or as life-sustaining as my devotion to you.

Thou art the star that guides me along life's changing sea;
And whate'er fate betides me,
This heart still turns to thee.

—George Morris

To see a world in a grain of sand
And a heaven in a wild flower
Hold infinity in the palm of your hand
And eternity in an hour.

—William Blake, "Auguries of Innocence"

(Note: Many couples *love* the symbolism of "hold infinity in the palm of your hand" as they present their wedding vows to each other!)

My bounty is as boundless as the sea,
My love as deep; the more I give to thee,
The more I have, for both are infinite.

—William Shakespeare, *Romeo and Juliet*

(Note: Couples who have included the beach or the ocean in their vows tell me that after their wedding every time they saw a beach or an ocean (or a lake or a sandbox), they thought of their vows and their wedding day.)

In nature, nothing is perfect and everything is perfect. Trees can be contorted, bent in weird ways, and they're still beautiful.

—Alice Walker

Every soul is to be cherished. Every flower is to bloom.

—Alice Walker

Use the season. If your wedding takes place in the tropical breezes of the summer sun, you can tie your vows in with the bright warmth of the summer and the memories you both have of summer getaways spent together and with your families.

An autumn destination wedding might bring you to a place that's rich with the oranges, yellows, and burnt siennas of fall foliage, with great vistas from the turning of the leaves. Your vows can refer to the colors you see, and how those colors reflect the end of one season (much like your single lives) and the beginning of another.

If your winter wedding sets you before majestic ski slopes, snow-covered trees, icicles, and gently falling snowflakes, you might use the symbolism of the snow. For example, how no two snowflakes are alike, and how no other love on earth is exactly like yours...or how your fiancé/fiancée is a true original, with no others like him/her on earth.

Even the rain can be a great motivator and perhaps a last-second addition to your vows if the skies open and raindrops fall on your wedding day. Rather than dampening your spirits on your big day, those showers can become a symbol of good portent for your marriage:

> They say that it's good luck when it rains on your wedding day...But we don't need luck. What the rain falling today means to me is that we're starting off our new life together with the washing away of our old lives.

Love comforteth like sunshine after rain.
—William Shakespeare, "Venus and Adonis"

Love is a fruit in season at all times,
and within reach of every hand.

—Mother Teresa

Mention the distance factor. Especially if you and your guests have taken two planes, a ferry, a bus, and another plane to reach your private island wedding destination, it's a meaningful tie in if you mention the lengths you both are willing to go to in order to join together as husband and wife:

I would go to the ends of the earth to take you as my husband...and as everyone here can attest, it seems like we have!

The guests enjoy a giggle of understanding, and you go on to recite your promissory vows.

Use your personal history with the place. For couples who may have gotten engaged on the beach at sunset, marrying on the beach as well is a very popular choice. You might choose to write vows that share with all of your guests just what it means to *you* to marry by the oceanside:

The last time we stood by the beach at sunset, you asked me to be your wife. And I said, "Yes." Now, as we stand at the ocean's edge once more, I am saying "Yes" to our promises to love one another forever, to be faithful always, to be partners and friends."

Multicultural Wedding Vows

To make your vows truly *yours*, you may feel strongly that incorporating shades of your ethnic or cultural backgrounds into your words—or rituals into your ceremony—would make your day complete. Since you are blending your lives together in marriage, it only makes sense to blend both of your backgrounds and values. Inserting ethnic proverbs, quotes, or sayings into your vows might be the perfect way to bring your two worlds together.

In this section, I've collected just a sampling of wording from a variety of cultures. I encourage you to use these as a jumping-off point as you begin to research your backgrounds for the ideal rituals, rites, and readings. For more details on your particular heritage and its wedding rituals, look for a book on your culture's practices, talk to a family elder or a leader of your house of worship, even contact a national heritage association for further guidance. Just as with religious elements to a ceremony and how this stage of research can bring you closer to your faith, looking into your cultural background can bring you an even greater bond to your family's most time-honored customs.

"I Love You" in Any Language

Even if you don't know (or don't care to know) the lineup of wedding rituals from your own ethnic background, it might be enough for you to just speak a portion of your vows in a language of your culture. (Especially if either of you have relatives who only speak their native tongue, they will appreciate recognizing some wording of your vows). You could repeat your entire speech in French, Russian, or Spanish, or you can take the easier path and just say "I love you" in that language at some point within your vows.

Here are some samples. I encourage you to ask family members for translations into your own language if your culture's equivalent is not mentioned here:

Spanish: *Te amo*
French: *Je t'aime*
German: *Ich liebe dich*
Italian: *Ti amo*
Portuguese: *Eu te amo*
Dutch: *Ik houd van u*
Norwegian: *Jeg elsker De*

Cultural Wedding Blessings and Proverbs

May love and laughter light your days,
And warm your heart and home.
May good and faithful friends be yours
Wherever you may roam.
May peace and plenty bless your world

With joy that long endures.
May all life's passing seasons
Bring the best to you and yours.

—Irish saying

Let's drink to love, which is nothing—unless it's divided by two.

—Irish saying

Married couples who love each other tell each other a thousand things without talking.

—Chinese saying

To love is nothing.
To be loved is something.
To love and be loved is everything.

—Greek saying

The heart that loves is always young.

—Greek saying

If love be timid, it is not true.

—Spanish saying

Shared joy is double joy. Shared sorrow is half sorrow.

—Swedish saying

Your embraces alone give life to my heart.

—Egyptian saying

Hold a true friend with both hands.

—Nigerian saying

Happy the bride and bridegroom, and thrice happy are they
Whose love grows stronger day by day,
And whose union remains undissolved until the last day.

—African-American saying

Translation, please?

Now, it's easy to translate *any* romantic sentiments into the language of your choice. Check out Google's language translator at www.google.com/language_tools for easy translations of words, phrases, even entire cut-and-paste blocks of text, poetry, and readings from English to Spanish, French, German, and others. It's a great way to repeat your vows in the language of your heritage!

Deep love is stronger than life.

—Jewish saying

Not until just before dawn do people sleep best;
Not until people get old do they become wise.

—Chinese proverb

Dwell not upon thy weariness,
Thy strength shall be according
To the measure of thy desire.

—Arab proverb

If you wish your merit to be known,
acknowledge that of other people's.

—Oriental proverb

INCORPORATING ETHNIC RITUALS INTO YOUR VOWS

In some colorful, cultural wedding ceremonies, centuries-old bridal rituals are enacted by the very modern bride and groom, as well as their families, as a tribute to their families' paths of origin. For many, standing under a chuppah as they take their vows, wearing traditional Asian wedding kimonos, or circling the altar a set number of times is the only way they would ever dream of conducting their wedding ceremonies. The ties to heritage are embraced by many couples who deeply honor their family and faith, and their marriage rites are filled with symbolic actions and words that have been practiced by generation upon generation of their relatives.

You might consider weaving these rituals into the vows you speak. Check out the following examples.

JEWISH TRADITION

For a Jewish wedding ceremony, it's traditional for the bride and groom to stand under a chuppah, which might be quite simple in its construction, or even custom-made to incorporate certain flowers or items that are precious to the couple.

As we stand under this chuppah today, shaded and protected from harm, and surrounded by the flowers of our birth months, I take you to be my husband. This chuppah symbolizes the new home and life we will build together, and I vow to you that I will always strive to fill both with happiness for all of my life.

For a less traditional Jewish ceremony or interfaith rites, the officiant may allow your own vows to veer from the traditional wedding ceremony script. When the groom stomps on the glass to the guests' shouts of "Mazel Tov!" you might follow it up with:

Now that we have broken the glass, we remember that sorrow always moderates happiness. We recognize the ending of our previous lives and start our life together anew, clearing away the shards of the past, and opening ourselves to the blessings of the future.

IRISH TRADITION

In an Irish wedding, you might exchange claddagh rings, a tradition that dates back to the 16th century when brides and grooms used the symbol of two hands holding a heart as their wedding icon.

I offer you myself as your bride, and as our wedding rings will depict and be an everlasting reminder to both of us, I offer you my heart to hold in your hands, as you have offered me yours.

NAVAJO TRADITION

In a Navajo wedding ceremony, tradition hearkens back to the days when the bride would wear a blanket or shawl that had been woven by the members of her community to symbolize the warmth and protection of marriage. You might choose to encircle yourselves as a couple with a shawl or woven blanket as drums beat a steady rhythm.

As our forefathers and foremothers did before us, we wrap ourselves in the folds of each other's protection, warmth, comfort, and love. As this covering is woven together of many threads, many colors and patterns, I offer you all of the colors and patterns of myself, and we'll weave mine with yours to create a new pattern that will comfort us and protect us all the days of our lives.

KOREAN TRADITION

In Korean wedding ceremonies, ducks play a symbolic role in marriage rites, since ducks mate for life. Use the image of ducks on your wedding programs and refer to them in your vows.

In my culture, ducks are used in wedding ceremonies as a symbol of everlasting partnership, because they mate for life. As I take your hand and promise you my heart and my love forever, my promise is that our marriage is for life, as well.

INDIAN TRADITION

In Indian weddings, a bride's hands and arms are decorated with henna designs in a symbolic marriage ritual.

The art I wear on my hands and arms may beautify me on the outside, but your love paints pictures of forever inside my heart. I am yours forever, in a love that is more beautiful than any painting or design.

In another Indian wedding tradition, the bride may be powdered with gold dust in preparation for her marriage ceremony.

You stand here before me, so beautiful, so adorned, dusted with gold powder as a tribute to my heritage. You couldn't be more precious to me. You are the gold that's in my heart, so beautiful, and I'm proud to call you my own. I promise to shower you with love, sprinkle you with adoration, and adorn you with my loyalty every day from now on.

Japanese Tradition

In Japanese weddings, the bride may switch from a traditional Japanese wedding kimono to a traditional white wedding gown, with the option to change her attire several times throughout the course of the wedding celebration. This symbolizes the changing aspects of a bride and of a marriage, much like "take me in all forms."

You are a woman of much beauty, always changing and always growing more and more lovely to me. I offer you myself in all my forms and appearances, all my demeanors and forms of loving you. Whatever you may be wrapped in, know that I am always going to be wrapped in your love and the promise of our long and loyal future together.

Scandinavian Tradition

In Scandinavian weddings, the bride wears a crown of either flowers or precious metals as she presents herself as a valued gift to her groom.

As I wear this crown, a moment I've waited for since I was a little girl, I honor you and promise to make you feel as regal and as valuable as you make me feel, to remember always what a precious gift you are to me, and to remember always how lucky I am to be married to a man who makes my childhood dreams come true.

GREEK TRADITION

In Greek weddings, the bride might stow a tiny square of sugar in her white gloves as a symbol of the sweetness of the marriage in the future.

May our life together be filled with sweetness, with the taste of kindness that you and I give so freely to one another. I promise you my life, my heart, my future, hand in hand with you. I promise to make each day sweeter than the one before it. I will love you always.

MIDDLE EASTERN AND ASIAN TRADITION

In some Middle Eastern and Asian wedding ceremonies, brides and grooms have practiced the ritual of symbolic bathing before their wedding ceremonies. Some cultures require the bathing of the bride's and groom's feet in a milk and honey bath, sometimes with flower petals sprinkled into the ceremonial bathing bowls. This ritual might take place before or even as a part of the marriage rites, to symbolize the washing away of all the steps and paths the couples have taken before this day, and to start them off "on the right foot" to a lucky and prosperous future.

My darling, we have washed away the steps of our youth now, the directions of our younger days and ways, and now with a fresh start on our journey together, I promise to take every step beside you.

In some Orthodox, Asian, or Middle Eastern weddings, the bride alone, or the bride with her groom, walk in a slow circle around the altar a certain number of times to fulfill a cultural symbol of honor toward the faith and promise of marriage. The number of "laps" a bride takes might be three, as an homage to the Holy Trinity, it might be seven as a matter of custom, or it might simply be one. This circling of the altar is a sacred part of wedding ceremonies in many cultures.

Now that we have circled our altar, walked our paces in honor and tradition, I honor you as my husband, and I promise to walk miles together with you wherever our paths may lead us, whatever the road may bring. I am your partner for life, your faithful wife, and your forever friend.

CATHOLIC TRADITION

In many Catholic wedding ceremonies, most notably Hispanic varieties, the wedding couple's hands are bound together with a rosary to symbolize their joining together with the protection of their religious faith. In some cultures, the practice of binding the couple's hands together might be done with a scarf, a gold-tassled cord, or a simple braid of fabric.

I tie myself to your faithfulness, bind myself to your wishes and goals, and connect myself to your heart. We are forever bound in love and loyalty, and I promise you all of myself as your friend, as your partner, as your wife. This bond between us will never break, even if it is stretched and strained sometimes, my promise is for life. I am yours always.

AFRICAN-AMERICAN TRADITION

In African-American and African-based weddings, the custom of "jumping the broom" dates back to the days of slavery, when brides and grooms would symbolize their bond by jumping together over a decorated broom. In today's Afro-inclusive weddings, couples still choose to honor their culture by jumping a broom after their ceremony is completed. To lead up to that moment, your vows might include:

In just a moment, we will jump the broom together. We will jump into our new life, our new world, our future filled with love and honor and loyalty and commitment. It's a jump I've been waiting all my life to take, a step I can't wait to take with you. You have my heart, my family's heart, and my full commitment always to make you as happy as you make me. So let's leap together into a wonderful future.

Chinese Tradition

In Chinese wedding ceremonies, the bride and groom bow three times to Heaven and Earth, to the Kitchen God, and to their family. Then they come together and bow to each other three times before the rest of the traditional Chinese rituals ensue. If the bride and groom choose to insert a bit of modernism into this hallowed set of rituals, vows that outwardly express the symbolism of the bowing might be:

> With my honor and respect, I bow to you.
>
> With my heart and my soul, I bow to you.
>
> With the promise of my eternal adoration and love, I bow to you.

To Our Love...

In Japanese weddings, the marrying couple take a sip of sake as part of their ceremony. Many other cultures include food and wine as elements of the marriage rites, whether it's taking a sip of wine or blackberry brandy, taking a bite of honeyed bread to symbolize sweetness and prosperity or fertility, a taste of sweets, or even a spoonful of pudding. If imbibing will be a part of your ceremony, then consider adding to your vows a tasteful addition such as:

> I drink to you, to your goodness and your kindness and your love. And I drink to our future together. May we always be as happy as we are now, and happier still in the sweet future we have before us.

Part Four:

Speaking Your Heart

Speaking Your Heart on the Wedding Day

The wedding vows you've written for one another are words you'll both remember forever. They'll be seared into your memory—recalled often in those proverbial "good times and bad" that will come along throughout the rest of your lives. You'll remember how you felt, the tears on your cheek, the look on your partner's face. You'll remember it all.

Now that you have the words, it's all about the delivery. *How* you say them is every bit as important as what you say.

So in this section, you'll get a few friendly reminders of how to make your words come out the way you intended them. The spotlight will be on you. You're standing in what will become an immortalized moment in time. How do you speak your heart when your emotions are flowing and all eyes are on you?

Read on and prepare yourself for the big moment...

Practice Makes Perfect...and Self-Confident

You read earlier that your best move is to practice reading your vows aloud at least several times before the big day. You're experimenting to see how those words come out of your mouth. Is anything a tongue-twister? Anything just a little too sappy to be *you*? Is your speech too long?

Once you have a near-final working draft completed, say it out loud in any of the following ways:

* *To yourself.* You might be your own best judge, so simply read your vows aloud and see if you like how you sound.

* *To another person.* Grab an impartial friend or family member and see what kind of feedback you get. Ask for complete and total honesty.

* *In the mirror.* Talking to yourself is perfectly fine in this situation! So stand in front of a mirror and see how it looks while you're reading your vows.

* *Into a recorder.* It could be video or audio, but this is a great way to listen to yourself reading your vows. Your thoughts might be, "Oh, I'm talking way too fast," or "Wow, that's perfect."

In the Moment

It's almost your time to speak at the ceremony. Your heart may be pounding already just from the sheer excitement of your wedding day, or you may be completely calm and together. Whatever your emotional state, this is the moment neither of you will

Memorizing Your Vows

If you want to memorize your vows instead of reading them or repeating them after the officiant's prompting, then give yourself a few weeks of carrying your vows around in your wallet to glance at a few dozen times a day, or listen to an audio recording of yourself saying your vows while you're commuting. The key is to give yourself lots of time to practice before the Big Day!

ever forget. So here are a few tips to make those wedding vows even *more* unforgettable—delivered with a deep and genuine sincerity your partner can feel. That's what's most important.

Make sure you're breathing! When you get nervous, your breathing might get shallow, and that can cause you to get spacey, dizzy, or to pass out altogether! So *breathe*! Slowly and deeply…make sure you unlock your knees as you're standing, and try to relax. That too is a dizziness factor.

Just before it's your time to speak, take a moment! Freeze that moment in time, the moment just before you make your vows. Notice how your partner looks, the smile on his or her face, and give a wink or a cute little nose wrinkle to convey to your partner a little extra sense of well-being. Too many couples get up there, freeze, get the "deer in the headlights" look, repeat their vows with little or no personality, and then hardly remember the moment afterwards. So grab that split second before you speak your vows as a private moment stolen just for the two of you.

Speak slowly and clearly. Be mindful not to rush through what you're saying. The speedy version is what trips you up, makes you stumble over your words, and the one thing you'll remember forever is that you messed up.

And if you mess up, just keep going! Laugh it off and start over. No one is going to blame you for being nervous. It happens to everyone, even those who speak publicly for a living. The less fuss you make about a messed-up word or phrase the better.

Use body language. As you hold hands during your vow recitation, give your partner's hand a few squeezes for emphasis on your most important promises, such as when you say, "I promise to love you forever." Look your partner in the eye as you promise him or her your heart. You can't be much more connected than that. So lock eyes and deliver your vows in the best way possible.

Don't worry if you shed a tear or two! You'll have very few moments in your life more emotional than this one, so if the tears flow, it's perfectly understandable. Tears of joy are a good thing, even if you're the groom. In fact, many wedding officiants and planners tell me that the groom tearing up is a great indicator of the couple's success rate. So don't be ashamed of those tears. Choking them back at the expense of your vow delivery actually takes away from the moment.

Really listen to your partner's vows. He or she has put a

lot into writing them, and they'll mean the world to you. So if you're speaking last, resist the urge to zone out while worrying about what *you'll* say next.

Know that the contents of your vows are not the only thing you'll get to say to your new spouse. This is just the public version, part of the ceremony. You can take some private time right after the wedding and open your heart even further.

Now *that* will really be a moment you'll remember forever.

Your Vows as Keepsakes

All along, you might have scribbled portions of your vows on Post-it® notes, cocktail napkins, or the back of the pizza delivery menu when inspiration hit. Then, you drafted your final vows on an index card and handed it to your officiant for reading during your ceremony. But keep in mind that your vows are the most important part of your wedding ceremony, so they're something you're going to want to hang on to.

While most couples just tuck their wedding vows index card into a keepsake box or photo album, others go to greater lengths to make lasting keepsakes out of them. In this chapter, you'll consider a few creative ways to make your wedding vows something to have and to hold forever and ever....

SOME POSSIBILITIES...

* Frame a decorative copy of your vows and display it in your home as an ever-present reminder of your promises to one another.
* Create gorgeous printouts of your vows and distribute them to guests as romantic and memorable keepsakes or favors.

* Roll them up like scrolls, tie them with a ribbon, and attach a bridal charm or a pouch of chocolates to each.
* Laminate them as wallet-sized cards.
* Make pretty bookmarks out of them.
* Include a full-page printout of your vows in your wedding album.
* Add a page featuring your vows to your personalized wedding website after the wedding as a forever keepsake online.
* Design your wedding day programs to include your printed wedding vows on the back cover, along with a lovely graphic, border, or photo of the two of you.
* Have your wedding videographer add the words of your wedding vows to appear as script on your wedding videotape. A great video edit can feature your vows in titles during a photo montage with a special soundtrack.
* Keep your printed vows as a keepsake for your children.
* Insert your vows printout into the plastic photo sleeve or frame that comes embedded in some unity candles.
* Use your printed, laminated, or framed vows in a special craft project, such as a first anniversary photo album, a mosaic tile frame, or a new family scrapbook; or have the words embossed or etched onto a first family holiday ornament.
* Print your vows out onto vellum, sheer, or

textured papers and include them along with your wedding portraits in your thank-you notes.

THE ART AND CRAFT OF VOW PRINTING

Most couples choose to print up their wedding vows using their own home computer and printer. Of course, you can certainly pay to have a professional printer, graphic designer, artist, or stationer print up your vows using thermography (the same process used for your wedding invitations and other official bridal papers), engraving (much more expensive, with raised lettering), embossing, or hand-drawn calligraphy. For some couples, this expense is a relatively minor one, and worth every penny for its artistry and elegance. You might even choose to use some of your wedding gift money for this service.

But if you'd rather do it yourself and add even more sentimentality to an already romantic keepsake, here are some production ideas to keep in mind.

* You can easily use your home computer's word processing program and clip art or graphics program to design your own vows keepsake masterpiece.
* Experiment with font styles and sizes.
* Use colored type, or two coordinated colors, such as deep hunter green for the title and lighter sage green for the vow wording, or deep rose for the title and a blush rose for the vow wording.
* Use word art to add a graphic element such as shading, flourishes, or three dimensionality to the type.

* Use beautiful, artistic paper to print your vows on. It can be a pale blue, pale pink, cream, lavender, or sage green paper found at any office supply store.

* Search at art supply stores for decorative papers with unique textures, shine, embedded rose petals, confetti, watermarks, and other special features.

* Look for exotic imported papers such as Egyptian cotton blend papers, gold-woven Moroccan paper, Japanese rice paper, and so on. Paper supply resources can be found online by searching for artistic paper suppliers or custom stationers.

* Hand-write your vows in a calligraphy style if you or a friend have a special talent for decorative writing.

* For perfect graphics, use rubber stamp art templates from the craft supply store, along with colored inks, wax seals or stamps, or a heat-embossed metallic printing process for a shiny finish.

* Purchase acid-free papers and photo albums to keep your vows page safe from aging, discoloration, or deterioration.

* Purchase a great photo frame to house your magnificently designed wedding vows page. Choose a beautiful frame that matches your home décor, or select a "talking frame" with a voice recording device that will play your own voices reading your vows whenever you press the button.

* Check out keepsake engraving specialists like www.thingsremembered.com, where you can have your vows printed for posterity on:

Picture frames

Jewelry boxes

Vases

Plaques

Or select phrases from your vows printed on:

Bracelets

Lockets

Necklace pendants

Money clips

Mugs

Champagne glasses

Wine glasses

Real-life Vows

The following are examples of vows from real-life weddings. The interfaith ministers and couples quoted here have submitted their most cherished words—and special memories—in order to help *you* craft your own unique wedding ceremony wording. Read on for more inspiration, highlight any wording that appeals to you, and turn down the page corner if something really speaks to your heart.

SAMPLE VOWS FROM FRANK JUDE BOCCIO, INTERFAITH MINISTER

I spoke with Reverend Frank Jude Boccio (www.judekaruna.net), an interfaith minister and Buddhist teacher who generously shares with you the vows of several of his recently married couples. Boccio offers these examples as a way of illustrating how you can work with your officiant to create your own vows, perhaps using samples he or she can supply from previous weddings. Officiants will often gladly supply you with recommended readings in addition to their tried-and-true vow templates.

You'll notice a supply of "response vows," where the officiant speaks the individual promises, and you both answer "I will" or "I do." Some couples prefer this method, seeing it as closer to the traditional vows of past decades, and also—quite realistically—easing the pressure on themselves to say a long and detailed speech. The choice of format is yours.

And now, Reverend Frank Jude Boccio offers you the same samples he offers his own couples:

Example #1:

Will you, _____, accept this man/woman, _____, as your husband/wife, joining with him/her) today in spirit; offering your friendship and loving-kindness; honoring his/her growth and freedom as well as your own; cherishing and respecting him/her, loving and embracing him/her in times of adversity as well as times of joy? If so, answer now, "I will."

Do you, _____ and _____, commit to nurture mutual love and trust; to aid each other in developing your physical, mental, and spiritual lives; to raise any children you may have with mindfulness and respect for the grave responsibility required; and to be faithful to each other, forsaking all others, and to be true companions and lifelong partners?

Couple answers, "We do."

Example #2:

_____ and _____, do you here in the presence of the world—as represented by those gathered here—declare your commitment to each other and freely choose each other as the one with whom you wish to share your life? Will you promise to care for each other through the joys and the sorrows, come what may, and to share the responsibility for the growth and enrichment of your life together?

Couple answers, "We do."

Example #3:

_____, you have embraced all aspects of my nature. You love me completely, for my strengths and weaknesses. You have given me the courage and faith to trust you, to let you love me as an entire person. Above all others, I take you just as you are, however you may change, to share my life. I gift you with my love and respect and I pledge to you my care and commitment of joy and sorrow, for today and throughout all of our tomorrows. So may it be.

A Word from Reverend Frank Jude Boccio

"The main thing to keep in mind is that this is where you give your word to each other. It is the heart of the marriage 'contract' where you stipulate, among other things, how you will behave to each other. There is no 'right way' or 'wrong way' to make a promise. Search your hearts, and the words will already be there."

Example #4:

_____, I give to you my hand and my love. I will respect you, honor you, and live my life openly with you. Through my love for you, I pledge to work to increase your happiness and to diminish your sorrows. I promise to cherish and protect you in good fortune and in adversity from this day forward. I promise to love you, to respect you, to laugh with you, and to soothe your tears. I promise to share my life openly and honestly with you and to encourage and nurture your growth. Together, we continue this journey of exploration, trust, and communication. I promise to savor each day, reveling in our loving relationship and in our pursuit of happiness.

SAMPLE VOWS FROM DEBORAH ROTH, INTERFAITH MINISTER

I asked Deborah Roth, an interfaith minister, relationship coach, and life transition coach in New York City (www.SpiritedLiving.com) to share some of the most memorable vows she's heard and helped write for her own recently performed weddings. As a relationship coach, Deborah knows the most fruitful promises that can be made at the start of a marriage, the true issues that rise up to challenge the newly promised, and the realistic vows that today's couples most often want to incorporate into their ceremonies. She also knows how original some couples can be—how they wish to use their own brand of spirituality and playfulness in their vows, and that couples like these often come to interfaith and nonreligious ministers for exactly this kind of freedom with their wedding words. Here are some of Deborah's top picks, as well as a little bit about the weddings themselves.

The wedding of Elana and Tyler

Elana and Tyler express in their vows the wonder of love discovered after a lengthy period of searching for one true partner. They express their gratitude for one another, for reawakening each other's hopes for a happy marriage.

Elana's vows: Dear Tyler, I want to publicly acknowledge you today because it is your love, devotion, and nurturing that has brought us to this glorious and sacred moment. When you came into my life, I didn't think that I could make this commitment again, but your tenderness and playful spirit have helped to heal my heart and soul. And today I offer them to you as your loving and devoted wife. I look forward to sharing the rest of my life's adventure with you.

Tyler's vows: Elana, I want to publicly acknowledge you today because it is your love and commitment, sense of play and adventure, and warm heart that have brought us to this altar today. I had almost resigned my life to one of being alone, and then you showed up and taught me how to be a genuine and loving partner. You brought out my caring and my openness and showed me that it was OK to love you from the bottom of my soul. I am so proud and happy to be at this moment with you today. I give you my heart.

The couple then took turns saying:

Let us rejoice in each other's successes.

Let us comfort each other in times of sorrow.

Let our love for each other be steadfast and unwavering.

Let each of us hold the other to their highest.

Let us remember to always leave time for play.

Let us never take each other's love for granted.

Let us accept each other without judgment.

Let us revel in each other's sensuality.

Both: Let us be each other's best friend on this adventure called life.

The wedding of Marc and Lani

This couple's vows portray the true meaning of the modern marriage as a partnership, built on support for one another as individuals, the value of partnership, and a life filled with love and friendship.

Marc says: Lani, I am lucky enough to be standing here tonight and promise to stand with you always. You are my greatest love and treasure. I promise to stand in front of you when I can guide you into our future or protect you from harm that may threaten you. I will never let you fall behind. You are my best friend and partner. I promise to stand beside you through the joys, struggles, and triumphs that will be our life together. We are a team. I am your biggest fan and supporter. I promise to stand behind you when I can learn from you or provide support by cheering you on. I will be there if you should slip and need me to catch you. Standing in front, beside, and behind you—I will always be there for you. I love you.

Lani says: Marc, as I stand here tonight in front of our family and friends, I promise you always my love and friendship. I promise to be your friend. I will always be there to hold your hand. I promise to be your partner. I will plan with you a life that is fulfilling and I promise that our children will be raised in the image of our love. I promise to be your wife. I will always support you and respect you and be proud to call you my husband. I promise myself to you fully. I love you.

The couple then exchanged their rings as a sealing of their vows.

Questions of Intent

Wedding vows might be spoken in any ceremony as a question/answer session, where the bride and groom simply make their promises in agreement with the statements read by the officiant. Here is an example from Lindsey and Michael's wedding:

Officiant asks: Lindsey, do you come before

this gathering of friends and family to pro-claim your love for Michael? Do you promise to affirm him, respect him, and care for him during times of joy and hardship? Do you commit yourself to sharing your feelings of happiness and sadness? Do you pledge to remain faithful to him?

Lindsey says, "I do."

The officiant then repeats the questions for Michael, who naturally agrees the same.

Real Vows from Brides and Grooms
"Our wedding vows were to 'love, honor, and humor each other.'"

—from Judith D. Schwartz in Bennington, Vermont

Minda Zetlin, from Woodstock, New York, said that her now-husband Bill was initially skeptical about writing their own wedding vows, and kept jokingly proposing things like "I promise to feed your fish." But he eventually got into it. Here are the vows that they made at their wedding:

_____, you are part of my life forever. I will be your lover and your companion, be honest with you and trust you, and share my life with you, now and for the rest of our lives. From today on, you and I are family. My family is your family, and your family is family to me. Take this ring, as a symbol of all these promises, and of my love, and to bind our lives together forever.

Part Five:

Worksheets

Your Wedding Vows Worksheet

Your Opening Phrase:

Remembrance of Your First Meeting (e.g., "When I first saw you, I thought…"):

What I Most Appreciate About You:

What You Bring To My Life:

Quotes or Poetry to Include:

What I Promise You Forever:

Closing (e.g., "This is my solemn vow," "I will love you always," etc.)

Your Time Clock

As a test, read your first draft aloud and time the duration of your reading. Then look below to see where you fit into the "appropriate duration" scale:

Ten seconds to fifteen seconds: You can do better than that!

Fifteen seconds to thirty seconds: Just perfect!

Thirty seconds to one minute: You have a lot to express, so go for it! You're still in a good duration zone.

One to two minutes: Come on, you can narrow it down a little, right?

Two to five minutes: Someone likes to hear his own voice...

Five minutes+: You're just rambling now. Focus!

Your Wedding Vows Word List

NOUNS

Love Passion Devotion Romance Affection
Attraction Faith Friendship Caring Connection
Attachment Blessing Admiration Joy Charm
Tenderness Commitment Alliance Fidelity Fun
Compassion Gifts Gratitude Magic Beauty
Bliss Heaven Angelic Optimism Partner
Peace Serenity Perfection Promise Vow
Eternity Laughter Smile Embrace Heart
Harmony Happiness Highlight Honesty Loyalty
Faithfulness Respect Honor Humor Hope
Plans Dreams Desire Dedication Lifetime
Intensity Integrity Destiny Values Elation
Pride Priority Emotions Team Duo
Pair Pleasure Purpose Qualities Traits
Family Sanctity Blessing Sincerity Soul
Spirit Thanks Thankfulness Trust Universe
Vision Wisdom Wishes Warmth Worthiness
Decency Substance Mind Body Goals

VERBS

Adore Cherish Honor Treasure Admire
Join Marry Connect Give Devote
Demonstrate Marvel Amaze Bond Open
Overcome Embrace Laugh Hold Dedicate
Desire Delight Value Embrace Leap
Jump Soar Fly Inspire Suit (one another)
Communicate Provide Protect Guard Lead

Follow   Nurture   Radiate   Rejoice   Renew
Respect   Sacrifice   Immortalize   Emulate   Support
Unite   Uplift   Remind   Shower   Praise
Comfort   Celebrate   Satisfy   Defend   Dedicate

QUALIFIERS
Absolute   Always   Forever   Eternity   Endless
Ceaseless Never-ending Constant Gentle Generous
Giving   Genuine   Natural   God-given   Blessed
Meaningful Tender Unending Enduring Selfless
Eternal Everlasting Flawless Exquisite Lasting
Heartfelt Limitless Immortal Ideal Indestructible
Powerful Strongest Inspiring Infinite Matching
Serene Sincere Steadfast Sublime Immortalized
Permanent Precious Priceless Invaluable Pure
Rare   Radiant   Inspiring   Real   Refreshing
Sacred Selfless Meant-to-be Total Ultimate
True Spiritual Compatible Gracious Awesome

TITLES
Companion Partner Sweetheart Friend Best Friend
Soulmate Spouse Husband Wife Kindred spirit
Honey Baby Prince Princess My Everything
Queen King My Heart My Light My Joy
Knight Angel My Dream Other Half My Inspiration

A Note from the Author

Congratulations! You're well on your way to creating your wedding vows, the most important words either of you will ever speak or hear in your lifetime together. You've searched your hearts, perhaps borrowed the most famous romantic sentiments in history, put those almost indescribable feelings of love and comfort and bliss into words, and you're prepared to stand up before all of your closest loved ones and declare your commitment to one another. I know it's not easy to express such deep feelings if you're not the sentimental type, and I applaud you for the courage it takes to accept this task.

It's not often in your lifetime that your own love and beliefs will be celebrated so publicly (and with so much champagne!) and I encourage you to remember the importance of the words you've chosen. Now and in the future, remind yourselves how important it is to speak your appreciation for one another out loud, whether you're having a romantic dinner for two or surrounded by everyone you know. So hang on to this book and consider using some of the expressions, the poetry, the quotes, and perhaps even a little inspiration from some of these vows for all of your *future* expressions of love to one another. Drop love notes in each other's briefcases. Scrawl a poem on the mirror in lipstick. Use a phrase in your anniversary cards to one another. Or just say "I love you" whenever the mood hits.

If there's one thing we know now more than ever, it's that there's never a wrong time to express gratitude, promise loyalty, and appreciate those we love and those who love us. I hope this book stays with you and encourages you to keep your marriage strong with the showering of sweet sentiments and the memories of your wedding day vows.

I wish you a future filled with love and laughter, and a partnership that grows only stronger all the days of your lives together.

—Sharon Naylor

ABOUT THE AUTHOR

Sharon Naylor is the author of sixteen wedding books, including *Your Special Wedding Toasts*, *The Complete Outdoor Wedding Planner*, *The Mother of the Bride Book*, *How to Have a Fabulous Wedding for $10,000 or Less*, *How to Plan an Elegant Wedding in Six Months or Less*, *The New Honeymoon Planner*, *The Ultimate Bridal Shower Idea Book*, and many others. She is also the co-author, along with celebrity bridal gown designers Michelle Roth and Henry Roth, of *Your Day, Your Way: The Essential Handbook for the 21st-Century Bride*. She has written for *Bride's*, *Bridal Guide*, *Bride Again*, *Self*, *Shape*, *Health*, and many other magazines, and she is the online wedding questions consultant at www.njwedding.com. She lives in Madison, New Jersey, and is working on additional titles for the Sourcebooks wedding series.

If you would like to share your wedding stories for future editions of Sharon Naylor's books, or to learn more about the author, visit www.sharonnaylor.net.